OUR FATHER,
WHERE ARE THE
FATHERS?

Our Father, Where Are the Fathers?

Ernest S. Lyght
Jonathan D. Keaton

Abingdon Press
Nashville

OUR FATHER, WHERE ARE THE FATHERS?

Copyright © 2012 by Abingdon Press

All rights reserved.

No part of this work may be reproduced or transmitted in any form or by any means, electronic or mechanical, including photocopying and recording, or by any information storage or retrieval system, except as may be expressly permitted by the 1976 Copyright Act or in writing from the publisher. Requests for permission should be addressed to Permissions, The United Methodist Publishing House, P.O. Box 801, 201 Eighth Avenue South, Nashville, TN 37202-0801 or e-mailed to permissions@umpublishing.org.

This book is printed on acid-free paper.

Library of Congress Cataloging-in-Publication Data

Lyght, Ernest S., 1934-
Our father, where are the fathers? / Ernest S. Lyght, Jonathan D. Keaton.
   p. cm.
ISBN 978-1-4267-4587-4 (book - paperback / trade pbk. : alk. paper)
1. African American fathers. 2. African American families. 3. African American men—Family relationships. 4. Fathers—Conduct of life. 5. Fatherhood—United States. 6. African American mothers. I. Keaton, Jonathan D. II. TItle.
E185.86.L94 2-011
306.874'208996073—dc23

2011045533

All scripture quotations unless noted otherwise are taken from the New Revised Standard Version of the Bible, copyright 1989 by the Division of Christian Education of the National Council of the Churches of Christ in the United States of America. Used by permission. All rights reserved.

Scripture quotations marked KJV are taken from the King James or Authorized Version of the Bible.

12 13 14 15 16 17 18 19 20 21—10 9 8 7 6 5 4 3 2 1

MANUFACTURED IN THE UNITED STATES OF AMERICA

Contents

Acknowledgments vii

Introduction ix

1. Father in the African American Family (Keaton) 1

2. I Remember (Lyght) 19

3. My Father: A Personal Portrait (Keaton) 27

4. The Black Church Fathers (Lyght) 39

5. "Our Father" (Lyght) 65

6. "Our Father" (Keaton) 73

7. Father at His Best 83

   Appendix A. Bishop Keaton's School Paper 93

   Appendix B. Bishop Keaton's Funeral Memoir 100

   Appendix C. Bishop Keaton's "Man in the Mirror" Article 106

Acknowledgments

First of all, this book celebrates the literary partnership we had with Bishop Edsel Albert Ammons. Since last we put pen to paper, our retired colleague has joined the church triumphant. Requested to partner with us for this reflection on "Our Father," he demurred. "I'm just not up to it anymore," he said. Bishop Ammons laid down his pen to focus on equipping himself for the last leg of his earthly journey. Yet his storehouse of prayers, life, spirit, and witness hover over this book. Already an episcopal colleague, Edsel Albert Ammons became an Ebony Church Father to Bishops Lyght and Keaton in co-authoring *The Confessions of Three Ebony Bishops* (Nashville: Abingdon Press, 2008). We give God thanks and praise for his work among us.

Furthermore, we extend our gratitude to African American Fathers; those *missing in action* and those *present and accounted for*. In nuclear and extended families, as single and divorced fathers, stepfathers, those in common law arrangements, situational, surrogate, adoptive parents, and beloved father figures, they have participated and shared in the raising of the next generations. Even though we issue from divergent family types, nuclear and matriarchal, the mark of our fathers, church fathers, and father figures is upon us as dads and servants of Jesus Christ.

Again, we appreciate the assistance of Mrs. Diane Allarding, the Executive Administrative Assistant to Bishop Keaton of the Michigan Area. She ably assisted in the first stages of the project. The new Administrative Assistant, Mrs. Deana E. Nelson, has been very helpful in preparing a final manuscript for the publisher.

Last but not least, we humbly acknowledge the example of the relationship between God and God's Son, Jesus Christ. Together, they create a paradigm of living worth emulating. They love each other. They love the world. And they partner to make the world a better place in this age and the age to come. Our meager words are an attempt to do the same. In our parenting roles, we join God the Father and God the Son in the renewing of our world so that abundant life for the family of God becomes real. And so we pray, "Thy kingdom come. Thy will be done in earth, as it is in heaven" (Matthew 6:10 KJV).

Ernest S. Lyght
Jonathan D. Keaton

Introduction

As the authors of this book, our role as fathers unites our mutual concerns about and our affirmation of fatherhood. Fatherhood comes from God, who created humankind in God's image. God has blessed each of us with children, thus enabling us to experience firsthand the responsibilities, the trials, and the joys of fatherhood. Although our experiences with our earthly fathers were different, we each have been nurtured by our common faith in the God who created us.

From a human perspective, our biological fatherhood is nurtured and ordered by the fatherhood of God. "See what love the Father has given us, that we should be called children of God; and that is what we are" (1 John 3:1). This God loved the world so much that we were given God's son, Jesus, who dwelled among us. So great was Jesus' love for humankind that he sacrificed his life for us. In giving his life for us, he taught us to live the way, the truth, and the life.

How then should we live? Jesus gives us some clues. He told the parable of the Prodigal Son, a father's son who left home and squandered his inheritance while living in an irresponsible manner. When he finally came to his senses, he decided to go home to his father, who welcomed him home with open arms and displayed the extravagant dimensions of a father's unselfish love. That is the way that God loves all the children of God. We live, therefore, as the children of God.

Introduction

As God's children, we "believe in God, the Father Almighty, creator of heaven and earth."[1] This creedal statement has been the church's confession of faith for several centuries. This belief and trust in the fatherhood of God provides the theological foundation for being a committed father in the context of today's church and community. With this faith we tell the story of our fathers, and dare to suggest some notions for nurturing fatherhood in our churches and practicing fatherhood in an informed and trustworthy manner.

There is, however, a sociological question that plagues our society: Where are the fathers? In the context of the local church, we ask a similar question: Where are the men? Far too often, we find that the fathers are missing from their families. In the African American community in particular, numerous men are missing. Some are hooked on drugs, in prison, or voluntarily absent. Other fathers are missing because they were killed defending America in war, are divorced and providing child support, are unemployed, never married the mother of their child, or died prematurely from disease or an accident.

Our expressions about fatherhood are not couched in any naive notions. We are compelled to confront certain realities, positive and negative. Our ideas have their roots in our Christian faith, as informed by Scripture, tradition, reason, and experience. We are also informed by the church fathers that we have encountered from the beginning of our nurturing experiences in The United Methodist Church. We confess, however, that our individual experiences as fathers have helped to shape our ideas. We, therefore, as brothers in Christ, share our thoughts as an offering to the whole United Methodist Church and beyond.

Ernest S. Lyght

Note

1. "The Apostles' Creed, Ecumenical Version," *The United Methodist Hymnal* (Nashville: The United Methodist Publishing House, 1989), 882.

CHAPTER ONE
Father in the African American Family

Jonathan D. Keaton

"I've been 'buked and I've been scorned..."[1]

The excerpt above comes from a famous Negro Spiritual. It speaks volumes regarding the sojourn of Black Folk in America. Our days of enslavement and so-called decades of freedom yield the same witness. Waves of negativity constantly flow over, around, under, and through the souls and spirits of Black Folk. Sad to say, the image of African Americans in America is not good. Compared to the dominant community, African Americans are said to have the highest rates of absentee fathers and unwed mothers. Poverty, poor education, mis-education, a disproportionate amount of Black males in the prison system, high unemployment, and poor health care have been identified as catalysts or causes for these dilemmas in the Black family. Many have argued that the African American father is the prime culprit. As a result, put-downs, blame, searing critiques, and outright disgust have rained down from observers and critics who remain convinced that the Black community and its leaders are totally responsible for these longstanding problems.

This pervasive myth has been challenged time and again. Obscuring the vision of those inside and outside the Black community are the facts of African American life. Some Black Folk have accepted some responsibility for these problems and sought solutions to them. Others have not. Also, truthtellers of American history have recognized that slavery and her children have had a deleterious effect on the Black family and the Black father. They have kept the concept of a level playing field between the races a dream and a promise, nothing more—just like "40 acres and a mule."

Looking through a glass darkly, the African American father is painted in a more realistic light, both "missing in action" and "present and accounted for." Regardless of perspective, "I've been 'buked and I've been scorned" is a timeless truth evidenced in the sojourn of Black Folk in America.

Missing in Action

When Barack Hussein Obama was elected the 44th president of the United States of America, I didn't know that we both struggled to make sense of the absence of a father in our lives. In his first book *Dreams of My Father,* President Obama said he learned a lot about his dad through stories. Barack's mother and maternal grandparents used apocryphal and true narratives to give him a sense of his paternal "roots." However, Mr. Obama didn't bite his tongue when family attempts to explain his childhood years proved inadequate. He responded, "There was only one problem: my father was missing. He had left paradise [Hawaii], and nothing that my mother or grandparents told me could obviate that single, unassailable fact. Their stories didn't tell me why he had left. They couldn't describe what it might have been like had he stayed."[2] Separated from his father at the age of two, connected with him through stories told by loved ones, feelings of sadness and joy aroused by an occasional letter addressed "Dear Son" from his namesake in Kenya; Obama's father was missing in action. A car accident killed his father when Barack reached the age of twenty-one, nullifying any possibility that the president and his father would ever relate man-to-man. Yet time and circumstance have made his father's absence a reality to ponder.

On June 16, 2008 presidential nominee Barack Obama spoke at the Apostolic Church of God in Chicago. It was Father's Day. Affirmation and challenge characterized his speech. Mr. Obama emphasized the importance of parental involvement in the lives of children. Also, he recalled how his life had been affected by his father's absence. Fortunately, his maternal grandparents stepped in to provide nurture and direction. This childhood experience led him to "break the cycle... and resolve to be a good father to [his] girls."[3] Connecting with some of his pain, Mr. Obama addressed Black fathers in general. "Black fathers... are missing from too many lives and too many homes," he said. "They have abandoned their responsibilities, acting like boys instead of men."[4] Those remarks reignited a long-standing discussion concerning ways to address the absence of the African American father.

In the MSNBC online report of Mr. Obama's speech, no specifics were offered as to what those "abandoned responsibilities" might be. A number of classic reasons are usually cited for the absence of the African American father:

First, a divorce has occurred. Legal obligations like child support, alimony, and visitation rights may not be fulfilled on a timely basis. Sometimes, they are ignored or resisted by the father, leading to pejorative terms like "deadbeat" or "no good" dad.

Second, the birthrate of illegitimate children is high among African American families.

Third, a disproportionate number of young Black males fill our prisons.

Fourth, homicides in the Black community have claimed countless young lives.

Fifth, unemployment and under-employment have wreaked havoc within the African American family. Allison Horton offers this observation, "job loss, decreasing work hours and personal family and health crises contribute to work instability. All these things are more likely to happen in families of color.... [Since the days of our American enslavement] we never started out on a level playing field."[5]

Sixth, the number of matriarchal African American families has continued to rise. In 2007, "49.4% of Black households were headed by single women."[6] These unmarried women or matriarchs have raised and nurtured the children in light of searing criticism. In the 1965 Moynihan Report on the Negro Family, matriarchal families were demonized for the following reasons: (a) they contribute to the breakdown of the Black nuclear family, (b) they weaken the ability of the father to function as an authority figure, (c) even worse, "the matriarchal family is said to be the paradigm for understanding the social and economic disintegration of...twentieth century black life."[7]

What I have just reported about matriarchal families has grieved me much. I, along with millions of others, was born into a matriarchal family. That status has subjected me to categorizations, so-called pathologies, and put downs. Those in my category will continue to face these issues as long as we live. And yet, I've wondered if a family structure created by necessity or by the vicissitudes of life is one of God's gifts to the people of God. In the ideal world, Mom and Dad ought to be together raising children in the context of a nuclear family. But life has never truly fit into neat categories.

The ascendance of matriarchy became another way to raise a family when circumstance meant the absence of a father in the home. That said, super soul singer Alicia Keys was roundly criticized when she said she was "blessed to be raised in a broken home." Alicia's dad left her mother when Alicia was two. Instead of affirming what one matriarchal family has produced out of necessity, the critic offered the following. "Please Alicia, consider the kind of message you are sending to our youth. We live in a world where 70% of the kids born in our community live in single-family homes and then consider how that contributes to juvenile delinquency and packed jails! We've got to do better. And you would figure Alicia Keys would know better."[8]

The list of problems cited here has contributed to a prevailing perception that the Black family is in trouble due to the continual absence of the male parent.

American Slavery

When presidential nominee Barack Obama spoke to the Apostolic Church of God in Chicago, he offered another tidbit that made me wonder what stood behind his words. His Father's Day message on missing Black fathers carried an implicit admission that the problem of absent Black fathers is not exclusively one of personal irresponsibility. At least, here is what an article reported that he said. " 'We can't simply write these problems off to past injustices... those injustices are real. There's a reason our families are in disrepair... but we can't keep using that as an excuse.' "[9] While candidate Obama offered a clarion call for Black fathers to "act like men rather than boys," he admitted that the problem of "missing black fathers" has historical roots. He never said what they were, but I am convinced those "past injustices" were and are rooted in American slavery.

Sitting in front of my computer Friday, March 19, 2010, I got in touch with this sentiment while reading an old e-mail somebody sent me in 2004. "This was once our resume," it declared. My eyes fell on the headline: *"Public Sale of Negroes by Richard Clagett....March 5, 1833...in Charleston, South Carolina. Lots of Negroes, mostly house servants, some for field work,"* will be sold.[10] Turned off, I turned away when I first received the message. Its truth was too much for me to bear. I didn't want to think about what really happened to the African American family in America. At the same time, the facts of the public sale reminded me of the torture and torment undergone by my forefathers and foremothers in order to deliver me to the twentieth and twenty-first centuries. For some reason, I refused to delete or read the e-mail. There it stayed on my computer until this current book project with my friend Bishop Ernest Shaw Lyght nudged me into confronting a history connected to the Black father in the African American family.

Richard Clagett's ad was revelatory. Who would be sold and what Clagett thought about Negroes represented a large segment of the American mindset. Key phrases and descriptions were used to whet the appetite of potential buyers who saw Negroes as chattel. Clagett advertised:

> A valuable Negro woman.... She has four children, one a girl about 13 years of age, another 7, a boy about 5, and an infant 11 months old. 2 of the children will be sold with the mother, the others separately, if it best suits the purchaser.... A very valuable Blacksmith, wife and daughters... 12 and 10 years old have been brought up as house servants, and as such are very valuable.... 2 likely young negro wenches, one of whom is 16 the other 13, both of whom have been taught and accustomed to the duties of house servants.... The 16 year old wench has one eye.... A likely yellow girl about 17 or 18 years old, has been accustomed to all kinds of house and garden work.... A man 30 to 33 years old, who has been raised in a genteel Virginia family.... His wife a likely wench of 25 to 30 raised in like manner... [and] their two children, girls of 12 and 4 or 5.

Claggett adds this commentary:

> They are bright mulattoes... well worthy of notice of a gentleman of fortune needing such.[11]

Claggett's advertisement served as a microcosm of what dominated much of Black life in America then. Even worse, it exemplified the very antithesis of a core value of America. The famous 1965 Moynihan report on the state of Black Folks in America leaves no doubt. "The role of the family in shaping character and ability is so pervasive as to be easily overlooked. The family is the basic unit of American life; it is the basic socializing unit. By and large, adult conduct in society is learned as a child."[12] If that were true of America, why had she made people of darker hue a radical exception? Why had America used its legal power to destroy Black families while at the same time "'buking and scorning them" for not being "normal" and productive? If a family can be destroyed by any means necessary, part of the family or the whole can be rendered ineffective at best and pathological at worst.

John Wesley did more than write theology, preach 40,000 sermons, establish class meetings, and set the stage for a movement that has become a world church. To Wesley, slavery, especially American slavery, was repugnant. It was "the vilest that ever saw the sun."[13] In his paper *Thoughts on Slavery*, Wesley described practices designed to atomize the strongest of human bonds.

> When the vessels arrive at their destined port, the Negroes are *again* exposed naked to the eyes of all that flock together, and the examination of their purchasers. Then they are separated to the plantations of their several masters, to see each other no more. Here, you may see mothers hanging over their daughters...and daughters clinging to their parents, till the whipper soon obliges them to part. And what can be more wretched than the condition they then enter upon? Banished from their country, from their friends and relations for ever, from every comfort of life, they are reduced to a state scarce anyway preferable to that of beasts of burden."[14]

At that level, survival of the fittest becomes the focus. Yet, I have imagined my enslaved ancestors transforming and overcoming their lot with this affirmation: "Some family, parts of my family, or my people are going to make it. It may not be me!!"

The infamous Moynihan report of 1965 lifted up the effects of slavery on the Black family even though the institution itself supposedly died with the passage of the thirteenth amendment to the Constitution in 1865. Slavery fathered segregation. Like its parent, segregation promoted and promulgated the myth of debased family life for Negroes. The late W. E. B. DuBois reported on the portrait of Black Folk painted by the major newspapers of his day (between 1890 and 1910). They portrayed Black Folk "as ignorant, lazy, improvident, clownish, irresponsible, childish and criminal." Undoubtedly, this research and other data contributed to the famous line in his well-known book *The Souls of Black Folk*: "the problem of the Twentieth Century is the problem of the color line."[15]

One hundred ninety years after Wesley mused about slavery and sixty years after DuBois wrote on segregation, Moynihan's controversial report on the state of the Black family agreed with them. Commenting on the "Black Past Remembered," the report talked about (a) the deterioration of the Black family and (b) Negro protest against white discrimination in actions and attitude. Hardest for whites to comprehend is the following: "to perceive the effect that three centuries of exploitation have had on the fabric of Negro Society itself...consequences of injustices done to Negro Americans are silent, hidden, i.e., we'll talk freely about the Holocaust but not American Slavery." Here, says the report, is where the true injury has occurred.[16]

Injustices foisted on the Black community by Jim Crow, segregation, discrimination, and racism have had a devastating effect on the Black family. One can't routinely break up Black families at the auction block, violate their wives, treat them as chattel, bind them with unjust laws curtailing every aspect of natural freedom, block access to education, kill, maim, and destroy for the slightest wrongdoing over the course of three centuries of slavery—and almost two more under her reverberations—and wash one's hands like Pontius Pilate, blithely proclaiming that the Black community alone is responsible for all the dilemmas that beset it. Yes, many Black fathers are missing in action. There exist at least two reasons for this: their own irresponsibility and the forced destruction of the Black family engendered by slavery and its aftermath for profit.

At the same time, while *some* Black fathers are missing in action, countless African American fathers are present and accounted for. That has been the case since our arrival on these shores.

Present and Accounted For

To get a more realistic picture of Black fathers who are and have been "present and accounted for," one has to look for family typologies other than the nuclear family. African American fathers perform their parental duties in many contexts. Realities such as divorce, unemployment, illness, prison, and death force and require African American men to use whatever style necessary to get the job done. Hence, we have to look for men who are present and accounted for in nuclear and extended families plus men engaged in nontraditional patterns: single parents, stepfathers, men in common-law arrangements, situational or surrogate or adoptive parents, or simply beloved father figures.

Scouring the marriage records of the Freedmen's Bureau, Reginald Washington uncovered stories of enslaved fathers heading nuclear families. His article "Sealing the Sacred Bonds of Holy Matrimony" shared an interesting marriage saga that was a wonderful revelation. Ex-slaves Benjamin Berry Manson and Sarah Ann Benton White secured an official marriage license April 19, 1866. Prior to emancipation, they had lived as husband and wife for twenty-three years.

The Mansons had sixteen children, and the entire family journeyed from slavery to freedom. Ironically, three of their sons, John, Martin, and William, helped to purchase the family's freedom by joining the military. John and Martin fought in the Civil War in the Fourteenth Regiment of the United States Colored Troops. William served in the army with the famed all-Black regiments of the Twenty-fourth and Twenty-fifth Infantry, and put his life on the line defending the American West.[17] Like the Mansons, the Freedmen's Bureau helped hundreds of former slaves legalize their slave marriages. Sadly, slave marriages were typically reserved for house Negroes, not their colleagues, labeled "field Negroes."[18] Nevertheless, field Negroes followed the example of their counterparts in the master's house. Apparently, the Middle Passage, the auction block, whippings, rubbing salt and pepper in the bloody wounds of the freshly lashed, pouring hot wax on the skin, and chopping off ears for taking up with Sue or Sally or Bill failed to break the human bonds and dignity of those who decided to shape their own destiny or take matters into their own hands come what may. In life and death, African American fathers used any means necessary to keep the family together and produce a generation to continue the upward trek toward freedom.

In the North and the South, free Negroes and manumitted and runaway slaves established their families and raised children. To be sure, free Negroes eked out a living in communities where the dominant majority erected laws, rules, and attitudinal barriers to "keep them in their place." They failed. Free Negroes joined trade unions, served in the military, started their own businesses, built schools, colleges, and churches, and established family values that enabled oppressed Black Folk to survive and thrive. More important, Negro families organized to contend with slavery, segregation, and racism in the quest for freedom. And right in the heart of that struggle and stride toward freedom were a multitude of fathers. Famous for surveying a layout for the District of Columbia, Benjamin Banneker petitioned the president to get rid of slavery. Negro sailor Crispus Attucks was the first martyr of the American Revolution. Thousands of unnamed Black men followed suit. Thousands more fathers made a lasting contribution to the Black community and family: John Russworn, who founded the first Negro newspaper in 1827; William Still, who led hundreds of Negroes to freedom via the Underground Railroad; Dred Scott, who unsuccessfully sued the government for his freedom. Perhaps the most important father figure standing at the top of the leadership pyramid for free and enslaved Negroes was the Black preacher. He could be found in every Black community. DuBois called the Black preacher "a leader, a politician, an orator, a boss, an intriguer and an idealist."[19] For me, the Black preacher was a "father to the fatherless, a mother to the motherless, a comforter in the time of trial," a visionary who could conduct the living and the dead from hell to heaven in a word or an all-day worship service.

When we fast forward our reflections to current times, divorce, children out of wedlock, unemployment, and other factors do reconfigure the traditional roles of the African American father. The 2006 Oscar-nominated movie *The Pursuit of Happyness* is more than a rags-to-riches tale based on the life of Chris Gardner. His son, Chris Gardner Jr., came into the world out of wedlock, and eventually, the child's mother left their son in his father's care. How Gardner cared for his young son touched a compassionate nerve of most moviegoers. Homelessness, caring for a young child, looking for a job, and working are daunting responsibilities. Abandoning his son never crossed his mind. They slept in public bathrooms, train stations, the airport, and cheap flophouses. Finding "cheap but good" seemed nearly impossible, but Chris found it at a day care center named *Happyness*.

Occasionally, Gardner found food and shelter at Glide Memorial United Methodist Church. They cater to homeless women with children, not men; however, Pastor Cecil Williams made an exception for this determined father. Chris Gardner worked like a dog at Dean Witter, where building a client base phone call after phone call tested his resolve constantly. That resolve bent but never broke because of his son's timely testimony. One night in their first rental apartment after escaping homelessness, Chris bathed his son by candlelight because the electric bill wasn't paid. According to Gardner, his son stood up in the tub and said, "Poppa, you know what? You're a good poppa."[20] From that moment on, Chris never looked back. He recalls the promise he made to himself out of the wreckage of his own childhood without a father and his promise not to abandon his own son with this quotation on the cover of his book *The Pursuit of Happyness*: "There is one commitment I hold above all, my commitment to my son."

Paris Katherine Jackson echoed the same sentiment about her dad, the late, great Michael Jackson. Spontaneously offering a heartfelt testimony about her dad at the memorial seen around the world, Paris Katherine made a poignant and unscripted declaration. "Ever since I was born, Daddy has been the best father you could imagine.... I just wanted to say I love him so much."[21] Paris's loving statement suggests that Jackson historians and observers missed something extremely important about this famous man. They repeatedly report that his record production the last twelve years of his life was limited and not impressive. What they have missed is that, for the last twelve years of Michael's life, he was most productive as a father and single parent. Michael Jackson raised and nurtured with love Prince Michael (aged twelve at the time of Jackson's death in 2010), Paris Katherine (11), and Prince Michael II (7). Despite the critiques and controversies that surrounded the King of Pop, Michael managed to raise three caring, loving, smart, and well-adjusted children.

The Importance of Present and Accounted For

Given the foregoing portraits of parenting, the value of fathers engaged in the lives of their children may be evident. If so, it bears reiteration or amplification. From the Moynihan Report, other family studies, and what we know of our families, we know that absent abuse or improper behavior by their fathers, children are likely to enjoy a stable home life, stay in school and graduate, stay out of jail, avoid early pregnancies, develop healthy images of self-worth, and build caring and loving relationships with their dads or other father figures. The childhood years of First Lady Michelle Lavaughn Robinson Obama offer a classic example of an African American father who was "present and accounted for."

Craig Robinson, the brother of our First Lady, shared an informative tidbit with a reporter prepping to interview his sister. To really understand Michelle, he said, the reporter would have to know a little about their father.[22] Here, the brother testifies to what he already knows by experience. Between his sister and her late dad, there remains a special bond. Labels like "Daddy's girl" and "her father's daughter," while poignant, do not fully capture the symbiotic nature of their relationship. In the literature regarding Fraser Robinson III, we observe a daughter inspired and influenced by her father's life. He does not complain about his multiple sclerosis and its debilitating effect on every aspect of his life. Instead, he contends with its advance by striving to be a good husband, doing for himself as much as possible, going to work, and shouldering the challenges of child raising as privilege, not problem. Furthermore, Fraser Robinson extends his concern beyond family to the neighborhood and the African American community. He and his daughter participated in Chicago politics by encouraging folk in the neighborhood to vote. Unknown are the wonderful moments of struggle, encouragement, and love when Fraser's only daughter sat on his knee, heard her name called, or enjoyed a big hug. Also, Fraser's death and precious memories drove home how positive and influential her father's presence had been. It brought a profound conviction to mind. "I am constantly trying to make sure that I am making him proud," the First Lady said. "What would my father think of the choices that I've made, how I've lived my life, what careers I chose, what man I married?"[23] As the absence of President Obama's father symbolized numerous Black fathers who are missing from their children's lives, Mrs. Obama's childhood and adult years point to countless Black fathers who are present and accounted for in the lives of their families and children.

Two years before his death, the late Howard Thurman acknowledged one timely and paternal act of kindness that changed his life. It's recorded in his autobiography, *With Head and Heart*. In the book, Howard Thurman talked about the men in his life: his father, two stepfathers, and father figures such as his cousin Thorton, a medical doctor named Stocking, and others.

Like most parents, Alice Thurman wanted her children to get a good education. But the city of Daytona Beach provided public education for Black children only through the seventh grade. Because of Howard's academic success, the policy changed. Daytona Beach added the eighth grade to the school he previously attended. Yet Howard faced an even greater hurdle after eighth grade. Only three high schools existed for Black children in the state of Florida. None of them were in Daytona Beach. If Howard wanted to continue his education, he had to leave home.

The day arrived for the departure of this fourteen-year-old. He packed a borrowed old trunk "absent lock and handles." Because the trunk had no handle, the ticket agent refused to include it on his ticket, following shipping regulations. To ship it, an extra fee was due. All Howard had left was "a dollar and a few cents." Distraught, he sat down on the steps of the railroad station and wept like a baby. His dream was dashed. When a stranger approached the teenaged boy wanting to know what was wrong, Howard stopped crying and explained. The stranger was a Black man.

Filled with compassion for young Howard, the man became a Good Samaritan. "If you're trying to get out of this damn town to get an education, the least I can do is help you." With an unlit cigarette dangling from his mouth, the stranger grabbed the trunk, took it to the agent, paid the fee, handed the receipt to the boy, and went on his way. According to Howard Thurman, the man "disappeared down the track. And I never saw him again."[24] Yet, he never forgot him.

The stranger became an exalted father figure in Howard's life. How so? When the time came to dedicate and honor a significant person contributing to his book, seventy-nine-year-old Dr. Howard Thurman passed over a list of worthy prospects including his beloved wife and children, Howard University, and the Interdenominational Fellowship Church in San Francisco he cofounded. Thurman didn't select Boston University or the Cathedral Church of St. John the Divine, his father, his two stepfathers, his mother, or his maternal grandmother. Rather, Thurman honored an unknown Black man who helped him to pursue his greatest dream. The renowned Black preacher, philosopher, mystic, and author of many books penned eighteen heartfelt words about a Black father figure on a white sheet of paper: "to the stranger in the railroad station in Daytona Beach who restored my broken dream sixty-five years ago."[25]

Conclusion

Alas, "I've been 'buked and I've been scorned" is still sung silently in the hearts and minds of countless African American fathers. These men love their wives and support their children. They work hard and protect and teach their sons and daughters. Education and the church are key elements in the family, community, and nation they seek to build. Sadly, the faithfulness and responsibility of these African American fathers rarely make headlines. Media reports about unwed mothers, absent fathers, jobless dads, Black men in prison, and countless other negatives carry the day. In essence, the only news worth talking about and up with regard to the African American father seems to be the pathology of Black Folk. To such genuflection, may the truth be known!

Notes

1. Traditional spiritual (http://www.negrospirituals.com/news-song/i_ve_been_buked_and_i-ve_been_scorned.htm).
2. Barack Obama, *Dreams from My Father* (New York: Three Rivers Press, 1995), 26.
3. According to an MSNBC.msn.com report of Mr. Obama's speech at the Apostolic Church of God in Chicago, he spoke these words to the congregation on June 16, 2008 (http://www.msnbc.msn.com/id/25176204/).
4. Ibid.
5. Allison Horton, "Whites Four Times Wealthier Than Blacks," *Jet* (June 14/21, 2010), 11.
6. Patrik Henry Bass, ed., "Black Women's Agenda," *Essence* (September 2010): 221.
7. Daniel Patrick Moynihan, "The Negro Family, The Case for National Action" (1965). http://www.dol.gov/oasam/programs/history/moynchapter2.htm (accessed November 2, 2011).
8. A critique of Alicia Keys's positive feelings about her single-parent uprasing (http://dimewars.com/Blog/ViewBlogArticle.aspx?vn=Alicia+Keys+Feels+BlessedTo+Be+Raised+In+A+Broken+Home%3f%3f&BlogID=53ffc897-f2b1-44d5-9a0e-97d3785ca5cd) accessed May 14, 2010.
9. Obama's speech at the Apostolic Church of God in Chicago, June 16, 2008.
10. The e-mail was an ad for the sale of my ancestors. See http://digital.tcl.sc.edu/cdm/singleitem/collection/bro/id/250.
11. Ibid. The dictionary defines a *wench* as "a young woman," "a female servant," "a prostitute" (*Merriam-Webster's Collegiate Dictionary*, 11th edition [Springfield, Mass.: Merriam-Webster, Inc., 2004], s.v. "wench"). History shows they were all three.
12. Moynihan, "The Negro Family, The Case for National Action."

13. John Wesley, letter to William Wilberforce, February 1791 (http://new.gbgm-umc.org/umhistory/wesley/wilberforce/).
14. John Wesley, *Thoughts upon Slavery* (http://new.gbgm-umc.org/umhistory/wesley/slavery/).
15. William E. B. Dubois, *The Souls of Black Folk* (New York: Avon Books, 1965), 209.
16. Moynihan, "The Negro Family, The Case for National Action."
17. See Reginald Washington's article "Sealing the Sacred Bonds of Holy Matrimony: Freedmen's Bureau Marriage Records," *Prologue* (Spring 2005), 37:1.
18. Ibid., 1–2.
19. Dubois, *The Souls of Black Folk*, 308.
20. See "Chris Gardner Stock Broker—Pursuit of Happyness True Story," http://www.chasingthefrog.com/reelfaces/pursuitofhappyness.php.
21. See Appendix C, Jonathan D. Keaton, "Man in the Mirror," originally published in the former *Michigan Christian Advocate*, September 2009.
22. Melinda Henneberger, "Michelle Obama Interview," *Readers Digest Australia* (http://www.readersdigest.com.au/michelle-obama-interview).
23. Edwidge Danticat, Internet article on the father of Michelle Obama, *New York Magazine*, March 15, 2009 (http://nymag.com/news/politics/55372/).
24. Howard Thurman, *With Head and Heart* (New York: Harcourt Brace Jovanovich, Inc., 1979), 24–25.
25. Ibid., dedication.

CHAPTER TWO
I Remember

Ernest S. Lyght

Dad: William Lemuel Dewey Lyght, Sr.

I recall my dad with warm affection and fond memories. There are many things that I remember about my father. I remember that he would take us for walks. When I was very young, we would walk from our house across the railroad tracks to the campus of Maryland State College in Princess Anne, Maryland. He continued to take daily walks until he was no longer able to walk on his own.

Having been an athlete during his collegiate years, Dad sometimes would race with us. It was a long time before I could beat him in a foot race, and by then, he had stopped engaging in races with me.

During his retirement years, of course, he walked to the nearby Brandywine Park to talk with his friends and to watch the baseball games. While my sons, Eric and Erwyn, were youngsters, when we visited my parents in Wilmington, Delaware, Dad would take the boys to the park with him so that they could play on the playground equipment. He always did this without fail.

I remember that Dad had very big hands and broad shoulders, although he only stood about five feet eight inches tall. The same hands that he spanked me with were the hands that tended to my childhood scrapes and bruises. When we children got hurt, we always went to Dad for first-aid treatment. Then we would go to Mom to secure a dose of sympathy. Interestingly, Dad's hands were big, tough, and rough, while Mom's hands were gentle and smooth. We made the choice, and Mom affirmed the choice because she left the nursing to Dad.

I remember that Dad always got up very early in the morning for prayer, meditation, and study. Perhaps he was an early riser because he had to get up early in the morning when he was doing farm work as a child and young adult. He believed that the morning was a good time to be in communion with God. He was more of a day person than a night person.

Also, I remember that Dad always had a garden during our growing-up years. When we lived in Princess Anne, Maryland, he had three gardens, one behind our house, one on the edge of town, and one at my grandfather's farm several miles away. Dad would take the vegetables that he grew and do canning. He would preserve huge quantities of fruit preserves and jam. These were really good to eat. The gardening chores would be done in the early morning before the sun got hot.

My siblings and I looked forward to our visits to the Black college campuses in our region to see football games—Maryland State College, Delaware State College, Morgan State College, Lincoln University (Pa.), and Cheney State College. These experiences were our first introduction to higher education institutions. Although Dad dropped out of school for a time to help his family financially, he never gave up the dream of going to college. It was understood that we all would go to college as a minimum standard of our education.

The Early Years

Every now and then when I was growing up, Dad would tell me that he did not want me to have to go through what he went through when he was growing up and working to become a responsible adult. Life for him was difficult by every standard. He shouldered certain family burdens while striving to reach his goals in life.

My father, William Lemuel Dewey Lyght, was the son of Alexander and Julia Light. He was born outside of Cambridge, Maryland, which is located on the Eastern Shore of Maryland, on September 25, 1898. His parents were among the working poor, living on the virtual edge of poverty. While the land was a source of food in season, they worked various jobs for white people to make ends meet. Life was further complicated when Dad's father died while William was still a young child.

William was the middle brother in the birth order, between his older brother, Howard, and his younger brother, Ernest. When I was born, I was named after Uncle Ernest and Bishop Alexander P. Shaw; so my given name is Ernest Shaw Lyght. Interestingly, the three brothers died in the order of their birth. Another family irony was the emergence of some different spellings of the family name. Uncle Howard spelled his name Light just as his father had done. Uncle Ernest spelled his name Lyte, perhaps for business reasons. He named his dry-cleaning business Elyte Cleaners. Dad took the name Light and changed the "i" to a "y," because as he told me, "I wanted to distinguish myself from the sunlight."

Names, obviously, were important to William. Depending on how people addressed my father, I could tell in what time period they had developed a relationship with him. If a person called him Jim, I knew that the relationship was rooted in childhood. When a person addressed him as William or Bill, it revealed a fairly recent relationship. As a matter of practice, he was known as W. L. D. in church circles. To me, he was always Daddy or Dad. When my brother William was born, Dad became a "senior"; however, he rarely used that suffix in reference to himself.

In the presence of their children, my mother always addressed my father as Daddy, and he addressed her as Mom. Presumably these familiar salutations were for our edification: Thelma Attrue Julia, William Lemuel Dewey (Junior), Celestine Cornelia Sarah, and Ernest Shaw. As their children, we never addressed our parents by their first names. That was a matter of strict juvenile protocol.

During the early years of his life, Dad worked on several of the neighborhood farms. One of his jobs was working for a dairy farmer. Before dawn, he would milk the cows. After that task was complete, he loaded the horse-drawn wagon and delivered milk to a number of customers in the Cambridge neighborhoods. When this work was done, he would go to school. I heard him mention with gratitude that his teacher at that time would excuse his late arrivals because of his milk delivery duties.

Dad's first school experience took place in the Methodist Church building at the Mission, a small village near the "Big Woods" outside of Cambridge, Maryland, where my father grew up. His first teacher was his mother, Julia Light. This, of course, was a one-room schoolhouse experience. Without it, there probably would not have been an educational opportunity for him at that time in his life. When he was a teenager, he dropped out of school to help the family financially. During those lean years, Dad managed to save some of his meager earnings. He always taught us that we should save some of what we earned. If he made a dollar, then he would save some of it, rather than spend all of it.

The day finally came when Dad was able to go to the Princess Anne Academy in Princess Anne, Maryland. The academy had been founded by the Delaware Conference of the Methodist Church. The Rev. Kiah, a Methodist minister, was the principal of the school. Dad chose this school because he felt that it would provide a good education for him in the midst of a segregated society that offered limited public education opportunities for African Americans. The Princess Anne Academy provided a primary and secondary education for its students.

The Middle Years

Dad graduated from Princess Anne Academy in 1926 and entered Morgan College, which had been founded by the Washington Conference of the Methodist Church. At Morgan he majored in English. When he was not in class or studying, he attended to his campus job as a janitor. During the summer months he worked on a variety of jobs. One summer he worked in a stone quarry in Wilmington, Delaware. Another summer, he worked on the railroad outside of Wilmington doing track repair. His mother was not able to provide him with financial jobs, so these manual labor jobs provided income to help him pay for his college education. Dad was no stranger to hard work, and he was committed to obtaining a college education.

During his college years, Dad played tackle and guard on the football team. He first tried out for the football team as a student at Princess Anne Academy. He knew little or nothing about football; he felt, however, that if he made the team he would have a free ride back to his hometown, Cambridge, Maryland. Dad excelled in college football, and he was later inducted into the Morgan State University Football Hall of Fame. At the University of Maryland Eastern Shore, one can see his picture in a prominent mural in the university field house.

Dad graduated from college in 1930, and moved on to theological studies in the theological school at Drew University, where he graduated in 1933. He was the only African American in his class. During his tenure there, he became the class treasurer. As a seminarian he spent his summers in Spring Lake, New Jersey, where he served as the student pastor of the Black Methodist Church. He was pastor there for six years, including three seminary years and three college years. During the summer months, he worked as a gardener, caring for lawns in the area. The Spring Lake charge was a summer appointment only, because it catered to a summer residency population.

Although Dad was focused on his studies, he found time to court my mom, who was living and working in Orange, New Jersey, not far from the Drew campus. He would catch the Erie Lackawanna Train in Madison and travel to see his sweetheart, Attrue, whom he had met at Princess Anne Academy. They later married in 1934 and parented four children together.

Ministry

Immediately after graduation from Drew Seminary in 1933, Dad went to his first full-time appointment at Centennial Methodist Episcopal Church in Smyrna, Delaware. He married my mother in 1934, and they had their first child in Smyrna. I was the fourth child in a family of two girls and two boys. Dad's pastoral appointments over the years included assignments in Harrington, Delaware; Princess Anne, Maryland; Chester, Pennsylvania; Atlantic City, New Jersey; and Wilmington, Delaware. We moved to Wilmington in 1955 when Dad became district superintendent of the Wilmington District of the former Delaware Conference. After retiring from the district in 1961, Dad was appointed as pastor of Ezion Methodist Church and retired from full-time ministry in 1968.

Dad enjoyed the work of ministry, especially preaching and visitation. I can remember watching him pore over his sermon in preparation for the Sunday service. He would get up early in the morning for prayer, meditation, and sermon preparation, writing out each sermon in longhand on 8½ by 11 notebook paper. All of his sermons, however, were delivered extemporaneously. Visitation was a high priority for Dad, and he could be seen calling on his parishioners on a regular basis.

Dad was my pastor during my growing-up years until he became a district superintendent when I was in the sixth grade. I enjoyed his preaching, partly because I liked to hear him tell the biblical stories in his sermons. He was a conversational preacher, and he often quoted hymns and poetry. I learned a lot about the Bible by listening to his sermons.

Retirement

The year 1968 was a transitional year in the Lyght family. Dad retired from full-time pastoral ministry, and moved into a home that he and Mom bought in Wilmington, Delaware. For the past fourteen years they had been living in Wilmington, where Dad served as a district superintendent and later as pastor of Ezion United Methodist Church. I graduated from Drew Theological Seminary in May of 1968. Thirty-five years after his own graduation, Dad and Mom came to my graduation ceremony on the Drew Campus. Shortly after graduation, I attended the 1968 session of the Peninsula Annual Conference and Bishop John Wesley Lord ordained me as an elder in the church.

At that session of the annual conference, I was received as a full member of the conference and Dad entered into the retired relationship. He literally passed the mantle to me. The mantle was full of pastoral wisdom. First, Dad always told me to treat all of my parishioners the same way. Do not show any partiality. Second, he urged me to begin preparing for next Sunday's sermon on Monday morning. His aphorism was this: "If God can speak to me on Sunday morning, surely he can speak to me on Monday morning." Dad taught me that an extemporaneous preacher always prepares the sermon and writes it out in full, well in advance of the time of delivery. Third, Dad taught me that it is important to visit your parishioners, especially the sick and shut-ins. Fourth, by example he advised me that one should never ask the congregation to do something that one is not willing to do. Fifth, I was greatly impressed by his devotion to prayer, Bible study, and sermon preparation.

Dad continued to write many new sermons during the years of his retirement. He enjoyed sharing sermon ideas with me. We would talk on the phone about a variety of sermon ideas and approaches to a particular text. He was an inspiration to me, and he was my mentor in ministry. He would offer advice, but he always reminded me that I had to decide how I would do the work of ministry. He refused to tell me what to do or how to do things.

Now Dad enjoyed preaching. In fact, he was the best preacher that I have ever known. After he retired, he was free to accept the many preaching invitations that he received from churches from a variety of denominations. On many Sundays he would drive to a church and preach at the morning service, then get in his car and drive to another city and preach at another church in the afternoon. He preached his last sermon at Centennial United Methodist Church in Smyrna, Delaware, where he had begun his ministry as a full-time pastor. That sermon was preached about six months before his death on September 26, 1988, two days after his ninetieth birthday.

The Legacy

Dad's legacy to me was faithfulness in ministry and commitment to one's call from God. Dad was a mentor for me in ministry, and he was a pastoral model for me. He had a positive influence on me in his role as father, husband, mentor, teacher, and supporter.

Perhaps the most important part of this legacy is the relationship of fatherhood that he provided for me and my siblings. I am forever grateful for the positive relationship that I had with my father.

CHAPTER THREE
My Father: A Personal Portrait

Jonathan D. Keaton

"Sometimes I feel like a motherless chile, a long ways from home."[1]

Above is a line from a famous and familiar Negro Spiritual. In verse, my enslaved ancestors acknowledged their presence in a strange land—a land that was not their home—America. This verse expresses a greater pain. Their circumstances and consequences left my ancestors feeling like a child without a mother. I do not know the reality of geographic relocation or the feeling of being "motherless." I am not nor have I ever felt like "a motherless child." That is not the case with my father. When I think of him, I do resonate fully with the words, the outlook, and the emotion of the verse because "sometimes I feel like a fatherless child."

How is that possible? Father figures dominate my life experience. Most of them populate "the church triumphant." As participants in "the great cloud of witnesses," they continue to encourage me on the journey. Among them are teachers, prophets, and priests. There are barbers, doctors, dentists, an Army chaplain, and other military men. In that number, I know well a stepfather, an uncle, a father-in-law, and husbands of laywomen in my home church. Other father figures come from the ranks of seminary professors, bishops, district superintendents, pastors, and special colleagues. These men have taught me about fatherhood and provided positive role models for three score years and five.

And yet my book of life has numerous blank pages, particularly in the section marked *Father*. My inability to claim any occasion where I knowingly related to my biological father or engaged in discourse with him bears out the reality that I never called any man in my presence Dad, Daddy, or Father!! At times, this realization leaves me undone, silenced, with limited perspective and needful of a relationship that can never be. Why? My father is dead. Learning something about him firsthand is no longer possible. Despite a good measure of health and wholeness, the servant ministry of the episcopacy, the rich blessings of a nice family and father figures galore, "sometimes I feel like a fatherless child." The reader may see why from two sources: my mother's account of my father's absence and my own.

Mother's Account of My Father's Absence

In a phone conversation with my mother July 13, 2008, I asked the following questions.

"Where was I born?"

"You were born in the back room of Mama's [my maternal grandmother's] house. You were born March 30, 1946, at eventide. Your elder sister and brother—Sandra and Jeffrey—and Mama were there. An Anglo physician and nurse came to the house. I do not remember their names. The Black doctor in town was sick."

Even with all those witnesses, I do not have a birth certificate documenting my entry to the world. A record exists somewhere. I know not where.

"Did my father know of my nativity?"

"He did, but days later. You carry his surname Keaton along with Jonathan Doyle. His name was Clinton Keaton. As you know, we were not married."
"Did he see me as a baby?"
"Yes he did, days later. And he held you in his arms."
"Did I ever see him again?"
"Yes, when you were preschool age, about six years old."
"Did my father acknowledge me as his son?"
"He did."
"Did he provide financial support?"
"He did not."
"How often did I visit my paternal grandparents? You and Leola Keaton [my first cousin] have said that I went to their house."
"I don't know how often you went nor do I know if your father was ever there to see you."
"How did you and my Dad meet?"
"I am not sure but it was probably at work, long before he joined the military."
"Although my father got married and eventually left Ft. Smith, Arkansas, and moved to New Orleans, what did he know about me?"
"He knew very little."

It's clear I do not know much about my father or his family. It's also clear that my mother knows more than I do. However, she follows a tradition of "the less said the better." So, I live and have lived and functioned without ever knowing many things about my roots. Yet questions about my father persist. What drives me to know more about me is complex and is not always clear to me. One thing is apparent. I hope such exploration will bring a fuller understanding of my life as I have lived it. Also, it may lead me to new relationships within my paternal family. While I want to know more about my father, this quest is no critique of my mother or her choices in life. I respect and value her decision not to open past chapters of her life. More important, I thank God for the personal witness acknowledged above: "I am not nor have I ever been or felt like 'a motherless child.'"

My Story of My Father's Absence

When this Ebony bishop entered life Saturday, March 30, 1946, no doctor attended my mother immediately.[2] A mad dash to the Negro Hospital, Twin City by name, had been averted. I had come too quickly. The shotgun house located at 2003 North 9th Street, Ft. Smith, Arkansas, served as a birthing room for me and at least one of my younger siblings.[3] Mama (my grandmother) assisted her daughter with the births and the child rearing. Now she housed three young grandchildren. Now she tended to medical and physical needs of her eldest daughter. What I have laid out as a birth narrative may be accurate in part, but not in the whole. My mother has revealed only disparate pieces of my birth story to me. This much I have learned: I have no birth certificate, my father was absent at my nativity, and I never lived with him. Hence, I never knew him.

In kindergarten, first grade, and Sunday school, my friends and classmates used a word that was beyond my experience: *Father*. "My father did this or my dad did that," they said. Or they described a vacation taken with Mom and Dad, a fishing trip with Pops, or a Christmas present from Dad. Hearing these oft-repeated narratives set off a spate of questions in my childish mind. Did I have a father? If so, where was he? What was a father? Unknowingly, Mother provided a partial antidote to my speculation and the questions of my friends and classmates. "You carry your father's surname Keaton along with Jonathan Doyle," she said. "And your father is named Clinton Keaton." Yes, I had a father. Yes, I belonged. But where was he?

Selective Memory and Projections

In the first forty-three years of my life, I have no memory of my father's presence. Nothing of my father's preschool visit or being held as a babe a few days after my birth remains in my conscious mind. So-called assurances by mother and Leola (my cousin) that I visited the house of my paternal grandparents several times meet the same result; I have *no* memory of them. In passing, one family connection stands out. But it has little to do with remembering relatives. For a season, the shotgun domiciles of both sets of grandparents had green siding. Why I remember that one fact remains a mystery for God or someone else to unlock.

Like other children's, my growing-up years were filled with school and church activities—work, study, choirs, plays, graduations, vacations, parent-teacher conferences, youth meetings, Father's Day, and so on. To my knowledge, he never came around for any of these events. Fate never provided me the opportunity to say, "Here is my Dad." Ironically, a handwritten paper I submitted to my English teacher in high school presents a radically different perspective.

Our English teacher, Mrs. Bullock, gave us an assignment (circa 1960). Students had to write about themselves under the headings My parents, My ancestors, My sisters and brothers, Early school days, My first trip, My first party, My best friend, The most wonderful day, Christmas at our house, My likes and dislikes, Plans for the future.[4] Reviewing my response to questions about my parents at age fourteen was surprising. I wrote: "My parents are Mr. and Mrs. John Keaton. My father finished high school...my mother did [too] and went to college. The college she attended was Philander Smith, in Little Rock, [Arkansas]." Clearly, the line "My parents are Mr. and Mrs. John Keaton" is a statement of wish fulfillment and not fact. As early as I could understand, two facts of life were crystal clear. First, my mother and father never married. Second, they never lived under the same roof. Yet I wrote of them in my paper as if they were married, perhaps longing for a different reality. My teacher knew it was not true. By the mercies of God, she did not call me out privately or publicly. In Ft. Smith, Arkansas, the Black community was so small that everybody knew a lot of truth about everybody. At fourteen years old, yours truly dealt with the consequences of his absentee father in a paper for English class by declaring his parents were Mr. and Mrs. John Keaton rather than Euba Mae Harris and Clinton Keaton.

As teen years were followed by college, seminary, and marriage, the wish exhibited in my high school paper took a nosedive. Hopes for some real encounter with my dad resulted in disappointment, anger, and cynicism. To complicate matters, I could not properly complete any form requiring family history. Countless times, I left forms blank or wrote "I don't know." Denied what I assumed and perceived other sons and daughters possessed, a definitive decision arose in my spirit. I resolved to share the facts about my dad when asked—and nothing but the facts—until such time as a personal encounter with him provided new information. I jettisoned my dreams of a different kind of family history. I remained set in that state until a parishioner challenged my thinking three years into a nine-year appointment at St. Luke United Methodist Church on the south side of Chicago.

St. Luke UMC celebrated Mother's Day and Father's Day annually. I did all right on Mother's Day sermons. But my Father's Day sermons left something to be desired. Had not the late Mrs. Dorothy Casey asked for a private meeting after hearing my third Father's Day sermon, my education about how I preached on Father's Day would have been delayed. In private, Mrs. Casey spoke these words to me, "Reverend Keaton, for three years, I've heard you preach Father's Day sermons. They're all negative. On Father's Day, I come to church to hear my father celebrated. He loves me. He's done a lot for me. He supported our family, loved my mother, and continues even now. Stop generalizing your experience and pain of no father in your life as the circumstance for everyone in this congregation. It's not fair. And it's wrong."

I was stunned. But at the moment she spoke the prophetic words to me, the scales fell from my eyes. I had allowed my personal pain to spill out in my sermons. Remorse and repentance tore at my spirit as her eyes penetrated my conscience and consciousness. I apologized. She left. And I lost it. Alone, I suffered and grappled with the truth of her words ringing in my ears.

Her prophetic word proved to be a God moment. It was one of the best things that ever happened to me in ministry. Not only did I become one of the best Father's Day preachers at St. Luke, I entered a time of greater self-examination about my absentee father. Since I knew none of the reasons for his absence in my life, I let go of longstanding assumptions: (1) He doesn't care about me or my mother; (2) He shouldn't have married someone else; (3) He's to blame for everything. By then, I was looking back on a life filled with hardships and great blessings. For example, I was born a healthy baby. I survived many bouts of pneumonia. I received a good education. I was nurtured and loved by God, Mama, Mother, the Black Church, and a passel of father figures. I was married and blessed with children. I had a job paying enough to support my family. The inherent need to know my father had not kept me from climbing up the rough side of the mountain with a reasonable portion of success, health, and wholeness. Forgiveness had claimed me. The desire for a face-to-face encounter with my father emerged afresh. But the need to see him no longer carried the baggage of blame, disappointment, and cynicism. I just wanted to meet him—to hear his story—to learn something of his thought process concerning me. So I prayed and asked God to let me see him in this life and not just the next.

Friday, June 29, 1989, I returned to Naperville, Illinois. My week-long teaching stint at the Wisconsin Annual Conference School of Christian Mission had been completed. I had led a spiritual growth study on the Psalms. As I walked into the house, my wife informed me that my mother had called. Beverly said that my father had died, his body had been returned to Ft. Smith from New Orleans, and he would be buried the next day. After brooding over the news of his death, I decided to fly home and attend the funeral Saturday, June 30, 1989. A longed-for encounter between my Dad and me was more than a possibility; it was inevitable. If I made it home, he would be *present*. I made it home. And Dad was there; in a sleep that only God could shake.[5]

Surrogate Father

Ironically, the absence of my birth father or a father in my home added a few complications to my life. I became a surrogate father myself, by necessity. To raise us, Mother and Mama had to work outside the home. Mama did day work, and Mother waited tables at two or three restaurants. For a growing brood of children, I was expected to keep order in the house, watch over younger siblings, make sure chores were done, reconcile conflicts and break up fights, do chores, know where my siblings were if they were away from the house, and, if instructed, "discipline a sibling." Of all the surrogate roles the one I disliked the most was "disciplining a sibling." It caused inner conflicts. It pitted me against the role into which I was born, nothing more than an elder brother. I wasn't even the oldest brother; two other siblings were older than I. I don't recall the day or the hour when Mother, Mama, or both instituted this role for me, but it was a radical change. In one moment, most of my life seemed carefree. And in the next, it was burdened with major responsibilities. Looking back and beyond my own situation, I functioned like so many other siblings caught in the same circumstance; I took over many of the roles of a father.

Because mother sent us to a private, Roman Catholic school, she found a way for me to make an economic contribution to the family. A conversation with Sister Pierre resulted in a janitorial job at the grade school. Every day I worked after school to pay for my tuition. Play time after school disappeared. By the time I made it home, school work had to be done. Maybe some of my siblings needed help with homework, or Mother and Mama had something for me to do. On one hand, I did my job gladly. On the other hand, all work and little play stamped a dullness or melancholy in my character that remains to this very day.

I never completely understood why such a burden was laid on me. An elder sister and brother were available. They had seniority. But the matriarchs chose me. Perhaps written on my persona were the words "compliant child; he will do as we ask." And I did for the most part. Their orders, requests, and expectations were performed to the best of my ability. Being thrust into the role of father figure caused me to grow and mature, but it stole a portion of my childhood years. Despite the traumas and difficulties associated with my role as surrogate father, my sisters and brothers constantly remind me of how important and helpful I was to them. Even now, some of them look to me for support and help. And to some degree, when they yell, I still respond. Old habits and responsibilities are hard to break.

Stepfather

Through the years, stepfathers entered and exited the lives of our family. Mother married three times. Her first husband never stayed with us and turned out to be a bigamist. The second did stay in our home briefly, but I have no memory of him. Then Mother married Mr. Ellesworth D. Winton in November 1962. I was sixteen years old. Shortly thereafter, mother moved from Mama's house. She and my younger siblings moved in with her and her new husband. I remained with Mama. Thank God, Mother gave me the freedom to choose, and I stayed. I lost my surrogate father role as suddenly as I had gained it. I had served as surrogate father for a number of years and accepting or dealing with another radical change in my life—a stepfather—was more than I could bear. So I chose the less stressful thing to do, stay with my aging grandmother and watch over her.

Time and circumstance erected a relational bridge between Mr. Winton and me. We got along well. Although I never lived under his roof, I quietly accepted life as it was. If I could help the family or my mother in any way, respond to requests made by Mr. Winton, I did so. He had no financial responsibility for me; nor did I expect it. Long before Mother married my stepfather, Mother's financial dilemmas, membership in a large family, and the small amount earned by my grandmother for "day work" had taught me a valuable lesson. If something was going to happen for me that cost money, I'd have to work. Mother clarified this reality in a conversation about "going to college." "I don't have enough money to give you all the things you need," she said, "but I want you to have them. I don't have enough money to send you to college, but, I want you to go. If it's going to happen, you're going to have to make it happen. You have my love and my prayers." She wanted me to go to college, as did Mama. And I did not want to disappoint either of them. Another great load was placed on my shoulders. Why? Nobody could help me—not my absent father, my mother, or my grandmother. Devastated, I moped for a while. Things changed for the better when I realized, "I must tell Jesus!!!" Like Jesus, I have the best father anyone could have, but I have to share Jesus' Dad with everyone else. He is none other than Our Father.

Notes

1. Traditional, "Sometimes I Feel Like a Motherless Chile," *Songs of Zion* (Nashville: Abingdon Press, 1981), 83. Used by permission.
2. March 30, 1946, was a Saturday. Harry Truman was president. At the time, there was no vice president.
3. My mother lives in the house where I was born in Fort Smith, Arkansas. Mama is deceased.
4. See the school paper in Appendix A. My mother attended Philander Smith College one year.
5. See Appendix B for a memoir of my father's funeral.

CHAPTER FOUR
The Black Church Fathers

Ernest S. Lyght

Who are the Black Church fathers? They are the saints who provided the foundation for building the Black presence in The United Methodist Church and its predecessor denominations. These spiritual leaders were inspired by African spiritual leaders who came before them in time. Most of all, they were inspired by the teaching of Jesus Christ.

These persons were men of faith who manifested the kind of faith defined in Hebrews 11:1: "Now faith is the assurance of things hoped for, the conviction of things not seen." This was not a blind faith, but a faith that opened their eyes to live and do the gospel of Jesus Christ. They sought to follow the example of Jesus, so their mantra was grounded in the Scripture:

> Therefore, since we are surrounded by so great a cloud of witnesses, let us also lay aside every weight and the sin that clings so closely, and let us run with perseverance the race that is set before us, looking to Jesus the pioneer and perfecter of our faith, who for the sake of the joy that was set before him endured the cross, disregarding its shame, and has taken his seat at the right hand of the throne of God. (Hebrews 12:1-2)

The Black Church fathers were committed to Jesus and the church of Jesus Christ.

These Black Church fathers were anchors in the middle of every storm. They were characterized by three dynamics. First, they were keepers of the faith. They kept the faith in terms of their personal living, and they taught the faith as a part of the faith journey for the followers of Jesus. They interpreted the faith and protected it from erroneous interpretations and any attempts to discredit or disrupt the faith through the faith traditions espoused by the church. These Black Church fathers were Methodist to the core in terms of polity and doctrine.

Second, these church fathers practiced an evangelism of faith sharing. They were not ashamed of the gospel. They believed in a triune God, and the doctrine of the trinity was central to their faith sharing. Third, these Black Church fathers were doers of the gospel. Their Christian identity was never in question because of the outpouring of their love of God and other people.

The Black Church fathers are the men who helped to form and shape the Black Church that shaped me as a young pilgrim disciple in the Methodist Church, now United Methodist. Some of these men I met personally, while others I only heard about or read about. These church fathers not only provided a theological foundation for the Black Church, they modeled some of the best practices in Christian discipleship. The Black Church was a spiritual oasis and a refuge that sheltered both men and women in the midst of the storms of life that raged in the Black community and beyond.

From a personal perspective, the Black Church fathers who helped to shape the Black Church also helped to shape my life as a Black youth and young adult. Some of these fathers helped me to hear the call to ministry and to embrace pastoral ministry. Their intellectual and spiritual mentoring also was influential in shaping my formation for ministry. These spiritual giants shared their best practices in ministry. Their example has helped me to be the best that I can be in the practice of ministry as a local church pastor, a district superintendent, and a general superintendent.

In this chapter, I want to share some reflections on the Black Church fathers that I consider to be significant figures in the history of the Black Church, the Black Methodist Church, and the Central Jurisdiction of the Methodist

Church. There are other Black Church fathers whose stories are not included here but who held a prominent role in the history of the Black Church.

When we speak of the Black Church, we recognize that there were Black mothers too. Their story, although not articulated here, is an integral part of the rich tapestry that we know as Black Church history. It is this historical tapestry that we want to glimpse as we consider some of the Black Church fathers.

African Origins

According to Africa University's Professor John Kurewa,[1] Africans have always had a concept of God. This concept of God predates Christianity. The African slaves, who were introduced to Jesus during the days of slavery in the states, therefore, already had their own original concept of God.

Dr. Kurewa notes first that African people believed in one God. They did not worship multiple gods; instead, they looked to the one God who was creator and sustainer of their world. Second, African people had a doctrine of salvation. Salvation was rooted in their relationship with God, suggesting that they could not do or become anything without God. Third, the African people believed in life after death. There was something special to look forward to after life on earth.

African thought was decisive in shaping Christian thought in general and African American Christianity in particular. African slaves brought their religion with them to the shores of America. The Black Church, which emerged over time, has its roots in African religion. Among other things, it was the Black preacher on the southern plantations in America who helped the transition from the African continent to the American shores by continuously telling the African experience and relating it to the new Christian experience.

The African American slaves were introduced to Christianity by their slave masters. The slaves took

Christianity and aligned it with their own native religions. Under the oppression of slavery, as noted by Howard Thurman, the slaves took Jeremiah's question "Is there no balm in Gilead?" (Jeremiah 8:22) and turned it into an exclamation, "There is a balm in Gilead!"[2] It was this kind of Christianity, rooted in African religious thought, that sustained Black people in America.

The Early African Church Fathers

There were a number of early African church fathers; however, we will briefly examine just a few of them. As African Christians and theologians, these church fathers helped to shape the Christianity that later shaped the African slaves who were brought to America in bondage during more than three centuries of the slave trade.

Origen

First, let us take a look at Origen, who was born A.D. 185. Origen was a noted Christian teacher and writer of religious materials. At one time in his career, he headed the church's training school in Alexandria, Egypt. Origen wrote more than six thousand books and lectured extensively at Rome, Caesarea, and Jerusalem. Through his writing and lecturing he became a moral leader in the church.[3]

Tertullian

A second African church father, Tertullian, or Quintus Septimius Florens Tertullian, was born in Carthage (A.D. 150–230). He became a Christian in A.D. 193. Tertullian also trained in the law and Latin. Relying on his knowledge of law, literature, and philosophy, he became an ardent defender of the Christian faith. He defended the Christian faith against the pagan state, the Jewish establishment, and several heretical sects. His *De Carne Christi* was written to prove that not only was Jesus born, he actually lived and died and was raised from the dead. His book *De Oratione* provided an interpretation of the Lord's Prayer. Tertullian had a significant impact on Christian thought, long after his death.[4]

Augustine

A third African church father was Saint Augustine (A.D. 354–430), who was perhaps the most famous of the Black Church fathers. Some theologians would argue that he was the father of Christian theology. A brilliant student, Augustine majored in rhetoric and philosophy. At age thirty-three, Augustine was consecrated Bishop of Hippo. During his lifetime he wrote some ninety books. His two best known books are *The Confessions* and *The City of God*. This later book, written in Latin, was released in the early fifth century. Its multiple themes include issues concerning God, martyrdom, Jews, and other dynamics of Christian theology. The purpose of the book was to explain the relationship of Christianity with other competing religions and philosophies. Despite what might happen to the Roman Empire, Augustine wanted the Christians to know that the City of God would ultimately prevail. He drew a contrast between the City of Man and the City of God, always keeping his eye fixed on Heaven. *The City of God* had a deep and abiding impact on the development of Western Christianity. In this book we see the Christian dynamic of hope, which has been at the core of Black Church religion from the beginning.[5]

The Organizing Church Fathers: Those Who Left

When we review the history of Black Folk in The United Methodist Church, one sees that there has been a Black presence from the beginning of the Methodist movement in

America. This American participation was preceded by Black participation in the Methodist movement led by John Wesley in England. There were, however, African American Methodists who left the denomination, while others stayed in the denomination. Some of the men who left made significant contributions to the Black Church in general.

The Methodist movement in America began to reflect the culture of racism and segregation in its early days. There was a racial incident at Old St. George's Church in Philadelphia, Pennsylvania, that involved Richard Allen in 1787.

Richard Allen

It was prayer time at the Old St. George's Methodist Church on a Sunday. On this occasion, the sexton directed the Blacks to sit in the newly constructed balcony rather than the main sanctuary where they customarily sat during the worship services. It was alleged that not only were the Black Folk told to move, Absalom Jones was forcefully pulled from his knees in order to get him to move. When the prayer time ended, many Black Folk left the church together. The end result was that Richard Allen led a group out of St. George's Church and formed a new religious fellowship.

Over a period of time, Richard Allen moved toward the establishment of the African Methodist Episcopal Church. The first worship center was established on the corner of Sixth and Lombard Streets in Philadelphia. Bishop Francis Asbury of the Methodist Episcopal Church dedicated the new building, a former blacksmith shop that had been moved to the lot owned by Allen. The congregation became known as Bethel African Methodist Episcopal Church.

Allen eventually summoned a convention of Black Church leaders on April 9, 1816. At this convention, the African Methodist Episcopal Church was organized. The participating church leaders ordained Allen and elected him as their first bishop. Bishop Richard Allen was an opponent of slavery and a strong advocate for freedom. He was an organizer, spiritual leader, and one who enabled Black Folk to overcome and strive for freedom.[6]

Daniel Alexander Payne

Daniel Alexander Payne was a Black Church father who, like Richard Allen, left the Methodist Church. Born in Charleston, South Carolina (February 24, 1811), he was nurtured in the Methodist Church. Largely self-educated, Payne became a clergyman, educator, author, and college administrator. He later became a bishop in the African Methodist Episcopal (AME) Church. A cofounder of Wilberforce University in Ohio, he became its first president.

Payne joined the AME Church in 1842. He decided that he wanted to be part of an independent Black Church. This posture would enable him to continue the struggle against slavery and racism without compromise. He was a strong proponent of clergy education. He was elected to the episcopacy in 1852.[7]

Absalom Jones

Another giant who left the Methodist Church was Absalom Jones, who was born into slavery in 1746 in Delaware. He died on February 13, 1818. Jones initially served as a lay minister for the Black members at St. George's Methodist Church in Philadelphia. He left St. George's with Richard Allen, and they combined their labor to form a non-denominational mutual aid society, the Free African Society. The purpose of the society was to assist newly freed slaves in the Philadelphia area.

Absalom Jones founded an African Church congregation in 1792. This Philadelphia congregation became known as the African Episcopal Church of St. Thomas, the first Black church in Philadelphia. Ordained as a deacon in 1795, Jones was ordained as a priest in 1804. He became, therefore, the first Black priest in the Episcopal Church. As a gifted orator, Absalom Jones waged a vigorous fight against slavery during his lifetime.[8]

Although Allen, Payne, and Jones left the Methodist Church, they made significant contributions to the Black Church and the Black community and society of their time. Their legacy and influence continue to influence the Black Church and Black Christians. They are Black Church fathers who left and, in leaving, provided a legacy for the future.

The Organizing Church Fathers Who Stayed

From the beginning of the Methodist movement in England, there were Black Folk in John Wesley's societies. Although there was prejudice and racial discrimination inside the American church, some Black Methodists stayed in the church. These Black Church fathers are a part of the foundation of the Methodist Church in general and the Black Methodist Church in particular.

In his volume *Black People in the Methodist Church,* Dr. William B. McClain refers to "three exemplary evangels" who I consider to be among the Black Church fathers. The three evangels are Harry Hoosier, John Stewart, and Henry Evans.[9]

Harry Hoosier

Harry Hoosier, or "Black Harry" as he was called, often could be found traveling with the church leaders, especially Bishop Francis Asbury. He was a more popular preacher than any of these mentors. One historian has credited Hoosier with the distinction of founding Zoar Methodist Church in Philadelphia.

Hoosier was born in the neighborhood of Fayetteville, North Carolina; the date of 1750 is used as Hoosier's birth year. Little is known about his life because he left no written record. Hoosier was illiterate in terms of reading and writing, but he could preach the gospel with power and authority. From the perspective of evangelism, Hoosier inspired many Black Folk to accept Jesus Christ and to unite with the Methodist movement. It is interesting to note that he was never ordained, in spite of his public ministry accomplishments. The ministry of Harry Hoosier has been an inspiration to the Black Methodist Church, providing a foundation for pride and acceptance.[10]

John Stewart

John Stewart is remembered for his missionary work among the Wyandotte Indians. It is believed that he was a freeborn mulatto born in Powhatan County, Virginia, about 1786. His missionary endeavors took him to Ohio, where he worked faithfully as a missionary among the Wyandotte Indians. The Native Americans had a positive response to the gospel message that Stewart preached.

John Stewart was characterized as "the pioneer of home missions" by William B. McClain. Eventually he was licensed as a local preacher, and he preached in a manner that was not only appealing but also convincing to his hearers. Stewart died at the age of thirty-seven on September 17, 1823, having left his mark among the Wyandotte Indians and the Methodist movement.[11]

Henry Evans

Henry Evans also was known among the Methodists for his preaching ability. His appeal held for both Black and white folk who wanted to hear the gospel proclaimed. In the Fayetteville, North Carolina, region, he worked as a church organizer, ministering across racial and cultural divides.

Born free in Virginia, Henry Evans became a shoemaker by trade, but an itinerant local preacher by calling. It was in Fayetteville that Evans first preached to the slaves; but he later preached to the whites who had heard about his strong preaching from their slaves. Evans was once threatened by a local mob; but this incident did not abort his ministry.[12]

The Missionary Bishops

African Americans served in a variety of capacities as the Methodist movement grew and developed in America during the 1800s. In some instances Blacks attended church with whites, although they might have had to sit in a segregated section of the church. On the other hand, some Blacks worshiped in their own churches, while still others worshiped in their own set-apart denomination, such as the African Methodist Episcopal Church and the African Methodist Episcopal Zion Church. The Christian (Colored) Methodist Church came later.

The Methodist Episcopal Church did not have any Black bishops. The first Black bishops were elected to serve, not in America, but in Liberia. Because of the crucial leadership role played by these early missionary bishops, they rank among the Black Church fathers. The four missionary bishops in the Methodist Episcopal Church were Bishop Francis Burns, Bishop John W. Roberts, Bishop Isaiah B. Scott, and Bishop Alexander P. Camphor. These men were missionaries, pioneers, and trailblazers.

A missionary bishop was elected to serve, not in America, but in a particular overseas mission field as determined by the church. These bishops had full episcopal powers, but only in their residential area. They were not general superintendents as were their white bishop colleagues. These bishops received their support from the Board of Foreign Missions.

Francis Burns

First, Francis Burns (1809–1863) holds the distinction of being the first African American bishop elected by the General Conference of the Methodist Episcopal Church and served as the first missionary bishop in Liberia. Burns was born on December 5, 1809, in Albany, New York. Because his parents were poor, he served a period of time "in service" with a farmer and he was indentured to another farmer. He became a converted Christian at the age of fifteen and began preaching at age seventeen. Burns found a home in the Methodist Church.

After entering into the Methodist ministry, Francis Burns went to Liberia and joined the Liberia Conference in 1838. In 1856, the General Conference of the Methodist Episcopal Church created the office of missionary bishop. At this time there was a need for episcopal leadership in the growing Liberian Conference. The Liberian Conference chose Francis Burns as their episcopal candidate, and the 1858 General Conference consecrated Burns to the office of bishop. Bishop Burns died on April 18, 1863, serving only five years as an active bishop.[13]

John Wright Roberts

Second, the Liberia Conference chose John Wright Roberts (1812–1875) to succeed Burns. Roberts was ordained an elder in 1841 and consecrated as a bishop in 1866 in New York. Prior to his election, Wright served as the presiding elder of the Monrovia District. Bishop Wright, the second missionary bishop, carried the torch of episcopal leadership in a difficult area.[14]

Isaiah Benjamin Scott

The third missionary bishop was Isaiah Benjamin Scott (1854–1931). He is remembered as a theologian, educator, and journalist. He was consecrated as a bishop in 1904. Isaiah Scott holds the distinction of being the first Black president of Wiley College in Marshall, Texas. He was chosen by the Freedmen's Aid and Southern Education Society of the Methodist Episcopal Church in 1893. He also served as a local church pastor, newspaper editor, and presiding elder. As a journalist, he was editor of the *Southwestern Christian Advocate* in New Orleans, having been appointed in 1896. While serving as the resident bishop in Liberia, new missions were established and the Methodist membership grew significantly.

Booker T. Washington quoted Bishop Scott in a treatise titled *Is the Negro Having a Fair Chance?* (November 1912): "The fairest white man that I have met in dealing with the colored man is the American white man. He understands the colored man better because of his contact with him, and he has more respect for the colored man who has accomplished something."[15]

Alexander P. Camphor

The fourth missionary bishop was Alexander P. Camphor (1865–1919). The son of former slaves, Camphor was born in Louisiana on a sugarcane plantation. Camphor's formal education began in a Freedman's Aid school, followed by graduation from the New Orleans University, now Dillard University. After teaching for four years at his alma mater, he went to Gammon Theological Seminary in Atlanta, Georgia. After securing his theological degree, Camphor pastored in Philadelphia and later in Orange, New Jersey. In 1896, Camphor became principal of Monrovia Seminary in Liberia. Under his leadership, the school developed, and in 1904, the institution was chartered as the College of West Africa. In 1908, Camphor became president of the Central Alabama Institute in Birmingham, Alabama. His tenure was interrupted by his election to the episcopacy in 1916. Those persons who knew him described him as a scholar, preacher, teacher, and administrator. Bishop Camphor, who served in Liberia, was indeed a church father.

These four missionary bishops helped to bridge the divide that separated African American Methodists from their brothers and sisters who were on the continent of Africa. They demonstrated the ability of Black Methodists to hold significant leadership positions in the church.[16]

Trailblazers

When considering the Black Church fathers in the Methodist Church, the names of three trailblazers come to mind because they were the first African American bishops elected by the Methodist Church prior to the 1939 uniting conference. The three Black bishops elected on separate ballots and consecrated were Robert Elijah Jones (1920), Matthew Wesley Clair (1920), and Alexander Preston Shaw (1936). These bishops, who were not missionary bishops like their African American predecessors, had to function as resident bishops for the all-Black annual conferences in the United States. They were trailblazers who lived out their discipleship in a segregated denomination and continued to pave the way for African American Methodists. They refused to leave the denomination and remained loyal Methodists.

Robert Elijah Jones

Robert Elijah Jones (1872–1960) was born in Greensboro, North Carolina. Bishop Jones is remembered for his pioneering leadership in helping to found Gulfside Assembly in Waveland, Mississippi. This Methodist retreat center became a mecca on the Gulf of Mexico where Blacks could assemble for their own retreats. There were no other options on the Gulf due to segregation. This historic retreat center was mostly destroyed by Hurricane Katrina in 2005. The delegates to the 1940 Jurisdictional Conference of the Central Jurisdiction met in St. Louis, Missouri, June 18–23. Bishop Robert E. Jones in the episcopal address gave some cogent reflections on the status of inclusiveness in the church. To be sure, the Central Jurisdiction was a segregated ecclesiastical structure based on white racism and prejudice. The establishment of the Central Jurisdiction was a compromise to maintain "unity." Jones noted that there were certain virtues in the plan. First, The Central Jurisdiction had the same powers as the five geographical jurisdictions. There would be equal representation at the general church level on boards and other committees. Second, the Central Jurisdiction would have full constitutional powers. Third, the Central Jurisdiction would elect its own bishops who would be full members of the Council of Bishops. Bishop Jones was committed to attaining a fully inclusive church; but that would not happen until the formation of The United Methodist Church in 1968.[17]

Matthew Wesley Clair, Sr.

The second trailblazer was Matthew Wesley Clair, Sr. (1865–1943), who was born in Union, West Virginia. He was the son of former slaves, Anthony and Ollie Clair. It is reported that Clair was converted at the age of fifteen at the Simpson Methodist Church in Charleston, West Virginia. In 1889, he was assigned to Harpers Ferry, West Virginia, as a licensed pastor. His pastoral ministry was distinguished, and he is remembered for rebuilding Asbury Church in Washington, D.C. This elegant structure had a seating capacity of 1,500. Clair died in Covington, Kentucky, and was interred in Washington, D.C.

Prior to his election to the episcopacy in 1920, Clair served as a district superintendent in the Washington Conference. After his election, his first episcopal assignment was Monrovia, Liberia. It was a significant accomplishment to be the second African American, along with Bishop Jones, to be elected to the episcopacy. In a literal sense, Bishop Clair was a father of Black Methodism because his son, Matthew W. Clair, Jr. (1890–1968), was elected to the episcopacy in 1952.[18]

Alexander Preston Shaw

After the election of the first two African American bishops, it would be sixteen years before the third trailblazer, Alexander Preston Shaw (1879–1966), was elected to the episcopacy in 1936. Shaw was a distinguished pastor, editor, and bishop, who was born in Abeville, Mississippi, the son of the Rev. Duncan and Maria Shaw. His parents had overcome the impediments of being former slaves. Shaw graduated from Rust College in 1902 and Gammon Theological Seminary in 1906. He was ordained an elder and received into full connection by the Washington Conference of the Methodist Episcopal Church in 1910.

His pastoral appointments were Westminster, Maryland; Harrisburg, Pennsylvania; Winchester, Virginia; Little Rock, Arkansas; and the Wesley Chapel Methodist Church in Los Angeles (1917–1931). From 1931 to 1936, Shaw served as the editor of the *Southwestern Christian Advocate* based in New Orleans.

After his election to the episcopacy, Bishop Alexander P. Shaw was assigned to the New Orleans Episcopal Area (1936–1940), followed by an assignment to the Baltimore Episcopal Area (1940–1952). During this later assignment, Bishop Shaw was my father's bishop for twelve years. I was born during his tenure, and my parents, William and Attrue Lyght, gave me his surname as my middle name. Bishop Shaw visited our parsonage and preached for my father at the Metropolitan Methodist Church in Princess Anne, Maryland.[19]

Theological Foundations

The early Black preachers tended to be orators and not scholarly writers espousing a systematic theology. The Black Church has not produced a systematic theologian who would produce a text on systematic theology. For that matter, John Wesley, the father of Methodism, did not produce a volume of systematic theology; he did produce volumes of sermons and his brother Charles wrote hundreds of hymns. The theology of the Black Church has largely been couched in its hymnody, much as the basic theology of the Methodist Church is ensconced in its hymnody, especially the hymns of Charles and John Wesley.

Early Black preachers had a pastoral theology that was espoused in their preaching and experienced in their ministerial presence with the people. They sought to bring "a word from the Lord." They were preachers, teachers, counselors, pastors, prophets, and theologians. They were church fathers; and a father teaches you how to live.

Charles Albert Tindley

When one considers the church fathers in the Black Methodist stream of the Black Church, the name of Charles Tindley readily comes to mind.

Charles Albert Tindley (1851–1933) was born in Berlin, Maryland, in very humble circumstances. He overcame poverty and became a self-educated Methodist minister. Although his father was a slave, Tindley was born free because his mother was a free woman. He is remembered as a pastor, extraordinary preacher, poet, and songwriter.

After moving to Philadelphia, Pennsylvania, he secured a job working as a church janitor. He continued to acquire knowledge, teaching himself to read Hebrew and Greek.

While working at East Calvary Methodist Church, Tindley literally moved from the janitor's closet to the pastor's study when he became the pastor of the church. Under his pastoral leadership, the congregation's membership increased to several thousand people. A new sanctuary was constructed to accommodate three thousand people, and the folk would fill the sanctuary twice on Sunday in order to hear "The Prince of Preachers."

Charles Tindley, from practical experience, understood the troubles of life as experienced by the former slaves and the Black population after slavery ended. In order to describe and identify the harshness of living as Black Folk in America, Tindley used the image of the storm. First, Tindley's theology was rooted and centered in God. He espoused a God who is creator, always victorious, all-knowing, and able to deliver God's people. Second, Tindley's theology was Christ centered. He believed that Jesus died for our sins, and, in dying, set us free. Jesus, therefore, is constantly saving us. Third, Tindley's theology relied on a God who answers prayer. God is ready and willing to receive our burdens.[20] He shared his thinking in his hymn *Leave It There*:

> If the world from you withhold
> Of its silver and its gold,
> And you have to get along with meager fare,
> Just remember in his Word
> How he feeds the little bird,
> Take your burden to the Lord and leave it there.
> Leave it there, leave it there,
> Take your burden to the Lord and leave it there.
> If you trust and never doubt,
> He will surely bring you out;
> Take your burden to the Lord and leave it there.[21]

For Tindley, the key to prayer was the practice of taking one's burdens to God and leaving them with God.

Fourth, Tindley believed in life after death. Although life is difficult, there is a God in heaven who answers prayer. In answering prayer, God does not reveal an answer to all of our questions or take away all of our pain. God is with us to the end, and enables us to live each day. Consider Tindley's hymn *By and By*:

> We are tossed and driven on the restless sea of time;
> Somber skies and howling tempest
> oft succeed a bright sunshine;
> in that land of perfect day,
> when the mists have rolled away,
> we will understand it better by and by.[22]

There are some things in life that we just do not understand. We have questions and no answers. But a time will come when we will see God face to face and all of our questions will be answered by God.

Tindley wanted people to have courage in the midst of the storms of life. His hymn *The Storm Is Passing Over* encompasses a theology of courage:

> Courage my soul and let us journey on,
> Tho' the night is dark
> It won't be very long.
> Thanks be to God,
> The morning light appears.
> The storm is passing over.[23]

There is always calm after the storm. This is a gift from God. Charles Tindley's theology, which was imbedded in his hymnody, provided a sure theological foundation for the Black Methodists and other church folk, including the Baptists. His hymnody was a gift to the whole United Methodist Church.

Other Church Fathers

The Black Methodist church did not develop in a vacuum. It was influenced by the thinking of church fathers who were not Methodist but Black Church fathers in their own right. These religious figures had an influence on Christians across denominational, racial, and cultural lines. Two distinguished church fathers who fall into this category are the Rev. Dr. Howard Thurman and the Rev. Dr. Martin Luther King, Jr.

Howard Thurman

I remember meeting Howard Thurman while a student at Morgan State College in Baltimore, Maryland. He was the speaker for our religious emphasis week. I was in awe of his intellect, his charisma, his powerful preaching, and his mystic qualities. Howard Thurman (1899–1981) was a Baptist minister, theologian, prolific writer, philosopher, educator, and civil rights leader. During his distinguished career, Dr. Thurman served as dean of Rankin Chapel at Howard University (1932–1944); co-pastor (1944–1953) of the Church for the Fellowship of All Peoples in San Francisco, California (the first racially integrated, intercultural church in the United States); dean of Marsh Chapel at Boston University (1953–1965); and chairman of the Board and director of the Howard Thurman Educational Trust in San Francisco.

One book from 1949 stands out among Thurman's many writings, *Jesus and the Disinherited*. This small volume deeply influenced religious and civic leaders, among them the Rev. Dr. Martin Luther King, Jr. It provided an impetus for the intellectual integrity of the Civil Rights Movement of the 1950s and 1960s. Thurman argued that

> the masses of men live with their backs constantly against the wall. They are the poor, the disinherited, the dispossessed. What does our religion say to them? The

issue is not what it counsels them to do for others whose need may be greater, but what religion offers to their own needs. The search for an answer to this question is perhaps the most important religious quest of modern life.[24]

For Thurman, Love is the answer.

Martin Luther King, Jr.

Love also was the answer for the Rev. Dr. Martin Luther King, Jr. (1929–1968). Dr. King was the speaker when my brother, William, and sister, Thelma, graduated together from Morgan State College in 1958. William since has reminded me that we heard Dr. King talk about three kinds of Greek love—*eros, philia,* and *agape.* As King gave leadership to the American Civil Rights Movement, he argued that love must be the regulating ideal. We must learn to love our "enemies," even the oppressor.

Martin Luther King, Jr., was a Baptist clergyman and prominent leader in the Civil Rights Movement. King led the Montgomery Bus Boycott in 1955 and was a founder of the Southern Christian Leadership Conference in 1957. He won the Nobel Peace Prize in 1964 in recognition of his labor to end racial segregation in America. At the time of his death in 1968, King had expanded his work to include ending poverty and ending the Vietnam War.

This American martyr was born in Atlanta, Georgia, the son of the Rev. Martin Luther King, Sr., and Alberta Williams King. He graduated from Morehouse College (Atlanta), Crozer Theological Seminary (Chester, Pa.), and Boston University, where he earned a doctorate. King was a pastor, leader, author, and prophet in his own time. There was a bridge between Howard Thurman and Martin Luther King. Both Thurman and King were civil rights leaders. Thurman had been a classmate of tKing's father at Morehouse College. Thurman was a kind of mentor to

Martin, and Thurman was dean of the Marsh Chapel while King was a student at Boston.

Martin Luther King, Jr., has had a profound impact on America, the Black Church, and this writer. His dream envisioned a color-blind world, and he called on civil rights demonstrators to practice nonviolence while loving the enemy. Like Thurman, he taught us to embrace the poor in an effort to eliminate poverty. One thing that King said at the Morgan State College graduation in 1958 was that young people should strive to be the best. For example, if you become a street sweeper, then be the best street sweeper. Martin Luther King not only inspired individual youth and adults to be the best, he challenged and inspired a nation to be the best for our children.[25]

Contemporary Church Fathers

As we give further attention to the Black Church fathers, let's take a brief look at a few more contemporary personalities who inspired their church to be the best. These men were leaders in the Methodist Church, as well as The United Methodist Church. In their own way, they have made an indelible mark on the denomination through their vision, courage, and faithful commitment. From a personal perspective, these church fathers were an inspiration to me during my youth and young adult days and beyond.

James Samuel Thomas

Bishop James Samuel Thomas (1919–2010), who served as the resident bishop in the Iowa Episcopal Area (1964–1976) and the Ohio East Episcopal Area (1976–1988), was a major contributor to the dismantling of the Central Jurisdiction, a racially segregated unit in the Methodist Church. Bishop Thomas has told the story of this effort in his book *Methodism's Racial Dilemma: The Story of the Central Jurisdiction*. Thomas served as chairperson of the Central

Jurisdiction Study and Research Committee of Five. This group formulated the plan that undergirded the merger of the Central Jurisdiction's segregated annual conferences into the five regional jurisdictions that were constituted on the basis of U.S. geography. The Central Jurisdiction met in 1964 and the Jurisdictional Conference elected James S. Thomas as its thirteenth bishop with the understanding that he would be transferred to the North Central Jurisdiction. When Bishop Thomas was assigned to the Iowa Area, he told the Methodist folk that he had come there to be the best bishop that he could be. As a Black Church father, Bishop Thomas has inspired others with his faithfulness, gentle spirit, scholarship, profound preaching, and persuasive leadership.[26]

Roy C. Nichols

The first African American bishop elected by the newly formed United Methodist Church in 1968 was Roy C. Nichols (1918–2002). He was elected by the Northeastern Jurisdiction and assigned to the Pittsburgh Episcopal Area. His election demonstrated the willingness of a jurisdiction to disregard race and elect a distinguished church leader to the office of bishop. Bishop Nichols was an effective pastoral leader, an able bishop, an active community leader, and an extraordinary preacher. He was indeed a preacher's preacher, enlightening and inspiring his hearers. For a sample of his preaching, one can read his book of sermons, *Footsteps in the Sea*. In this book, Nichols proclaims and illustrates how God's power is at work in the global village. Bishop Nichols was a proponent of education and served several years as chairperson of Africa University's Advisory Development Committee. He also served a one-year term as president of the Council of Bishops. As a Black Church father, Bishop Nichols has inspired both ministers and laypeople across denominational lines.[27]

Earnest A. Smith

Another Black Church father was Dr. Earnest A. Smith, who died in 2009. As a layperson he served with distinction as president of Rust College (1957–1967) and as associate general secretary at the General Board of Church and Society (1966–1980). He provided a positive role model for hundreds of Black college students as a college president. He provided profound insights in the arena of social concerns and human relations. He will be long remembered by the constituency of Black Methodists for Church Renewal for his prophetic words in 1968: "Our time under God is now!" This emphatic statement continues to provide guidance and inspiration for Black United Methodist people. Our fathers play this crucial role of being those who inspire and guide.[28]

My Church Fathers

Let me conclude this chapter by sharing a few reflections about those persons I consider to be my church fathers in The United Methodist Church.

W. L. D. Lyght, Sr.

First and foremost was my father, W. L. D. Lyght, Sr., who helped me to hear God's call through his ministerial presence. He modeled excellence in pastoral ministry that was predicated on a love for God's people and God's word. He manifested powerful evangelical preaching. Also, he modeled administrative and organizational skills as a district superintendent. Most of all, he taught me to treat all people the same way.

Howard Cornish

When I went to college, I met the Rev. Howard Cornish, who was the college chaplain. Reverend Cornish provided an opportunity for me to be his worship assistant and liturgist for the Sunday morning worship services. He helped me to explore God's call to ministry; he encouraged me to embrace God's call to pastoral ministry.

Edgar A. Love

Bishop Edgar A. Love was the resident bishop of the Delaware Conference where I was licensed to preach. Each year at the annual conference during the service of ordination, Bishop Love would invite all potential candidates for ministry to come forward to the altar for prayer. In addition, he invited me along with other young people to attend his Christmas luncheon for ministerial candidates. At these sessions he encouraged the participants in our quest for ministry.

George Outen

As I was making the journey toward ordination, I remember two persons who had an influence on my journey not so much because of what they said but because of what they modeled as leaders in the church. First, the Rev. George Outen, who served as a counselor at some of our conference youth events, from my perspective, exhibited excellence in ministry. He was modest, talented, a good leader, and a gifted preacher.

Leonard Miller

Second, Leonard Miller also was a youth leader, among other things. I was impressed by his vast knowledge of The United Methodist Church. He could articulate the organizational genius of the church and why it was important to know the church's structure.

Prince A. Taylor, Jr.

Bishop Prince A. Taylor, Jr., was not my ordaining bishop, but he gave me my first appointment in the former Southern New Jersey Annual Conference (SNJC). I remember that he invited me to transfer my conference membership from the Peninsula Conference to the SNJC after my graduation from theological seminary. He gave me many words of encouragement and challenge. I will always remember our many conversations that continued until his death after I became an episcopal leader.

Notes

1. John Kurewa, "What It Is in Evangelization in Africa That Makes the Efforts Particularly Effective, and the Dynamics That Contribute to the Amazing Growth." Speech given at the Council of Bishops meeting ("COB Minutes," Maputo, Mozambique: November 1–6, 2006), 357–59.

2. Howard Thurman, *Deep River and The Negro Spiritual Speaks of Life and Death* (Richmond, Ind.: Friends United Press, 1975), 60.

3. Mark Hyman, *Blacks Who Died for Christ* (Philadelphia: Corrective Black History Books, 1983), 16–18.

4. Ibid., 18–20.

5. Ibid., 31–33.

6. J. Gordon Melton, *A Will to Choose: The Origins of African American Methodism* (Lanham, Md.: Rowman & Littlefield, 2007), 91–98. Richard Allen, *The Life Experience and Gospel Labors of the Right Rev. Richard Allen* (Nashville: Abingdon Press, 1960), 15–86.

7. Harry V. Richardson, *Dark Salvation—The Story of Methodism as It Developed among Blacks in America* (Garden City, NY: Anchor Press/Doubleday, 1976), 104–108.

8. Ibid., 62–75.

9. William B. McClain, *Black People in The Methodist Church, Whither Thou Goest?* (Cambridge, Mass.: Schenkman, 1984), 39.

10. Ibid., 41–46.

11. Ibid., 46–51.

12. Ibid., 51–54.

13. Melton, 260.

14. Ibid., 260–1.

15. Grant S. Shockley, ed., *Heritage and Hope: The African American Presence in United Methodism* (Nashville: Abingdon Press, 1991), 47,

58–59, 67, 77, 82, 86. Booker T. Washington quotation of Bishop Scott is from "Is the Negro Having a Fair Chance?" (http://teachingamericahistory.org/library/index.asp?document=1154, accessed November 16, 2011).

16. Shockley, 66–67. Alexander Priestly Camphor, *Missionary Story Sketches: Folklore from Africa* (New York: Easton & Mains, 1909), 7–10.

17. Richardson, 278–79. Shockley, 168–69.

18. Richardson, 275–76. Shockley, 88, 159, 161, 308.

19. Richardson, 274, 276. Shockley, 86, 88, 90. McClain, 90. J. Beverly F. Shaw, *The Life and Work of Bishop Alexander Preston Shaw* (Nashville: The Parthenon Press, 1948), 9–32.

20. Shockley, 94–95. McClain, 30–31.

21. Charles Albert Tindley, "Leave It There," *The United Methodist Hymnal* (Nashville: The United Methodist Publishing House, 1989), 522. Used by permission.

22. Tindley, "By and By," *The United Methodist Hymnal* (Nashville: The United Methodist Publishing House, 1989), 525. Used by permission.

23. Tindley, "The Storm Is Passing Over," *Songs of Zion* (Nashville: The United Methodist Publishing House, 1981), 58. Used by permission.

24. Howard Thurman, *With Head and Heart* (New York: Harcourt Brace Jovanovich, 1979), 31–100.

25. Ernest S. Lyght, *The Religious and Philosophical Foundations in the Thought of Martin Luther King, Jr.* (New York: Vantage Press, 1972), 17–27.

26. Shockley, 60, 141, 146, 163, 211, 298.

27. Ibid., 211, 296.

28. Woodie W. White, ed., *Our Time under God Is Now* (Nashville: Abingdon Press, 1993), 89–92.

CHAPTER FIVE
"Our Father"

Ernest S. Lyght

"Our Father in heaven, hallowed be your name."
—Matthew 6:9b

I do not remember when my parents taught me as a young child to pray the Lord's Prayer. It seems that I have been praying the Lord's Prayer all of my life. When I think of prayer, the Lord's Prayer is usually the first formal prayer that comes to mind. It serves as a model prayer for me. Every night, before going to bed, I prayed the Lord's Prayer. Every Sunday at the church, the congregation would chant the Lord's Prayer. Each Sunday at the dinner table after church, the family prayed the Lord's Prayer before my father offered a prayer that blessed the food. To this day, the Lord's Prayer is included in my daily prayer ritual.

My parents started me on the journey of learning to pray by teaching me to pray the venerable Lord's Prayer. It is this prayer that Jesus used in teaching his disciples the art of prayer:

> Pray then in this way:
> Our Father in heaven,

> hallowed be your name.
> Your kingdom come.
> Your will be done,
>> on earth as it is in heaven.
>
> Give us this day our daily bread.
> And forgive us our debts,
>> as we also have forgiven our debtors.
>
> And do not bring us to the time of trial,
>> but rescue us from the evil one. (Matthew 6:9-13)

Many Christians learned this prayer either in their childhood or during the early days of their pilgrim discipleship with Jesus. It is the prayer most often heard in the global village when Christians gather for prayer, in public and in private.

The Lord's Prayer is couched in the context of Jesus' discourse on public and private piety. Jesus admonished his hearers to be cautious, indeed reticent, about displaying their piety in order to be seen by other people. He warned against giving alms publicly. His advice was to give one's alms in secret, because the Lord, who sees in secret, would reward them. Jesus was concerned about the hypocrites who often engaged in loud public displays of piety.

Jesus did not stop with his rebuke about almsgiving but went on to critique the public prayers of the hypocrites who desired to be seen by other people. The hypocrites liked to pray not only in the synagogues but also on the street corners. Jesus countered this behavior with the simple admonition that whenever one prays, one ought to go into one's private room and "pray to your Father who is in secret" (Matthew 6:6a). Such a prayer posture garners the Father's reward. What is offered to the Father in secret is rewarded by the Father in secret. Personal prayer, therefore, is private and confidential conversation with God. To pray, then, is to "have a little talk with Jesus [and] tell him all about our troubles."[1] The assumption is that Jesus will "answer by and by."

Jesus also instructed the disciples to be brief in their prayers. He cautioned them about embellishing the prayer conversation with "empty phrases" (Matthew 6:7). This was the practice of the Gentiles, and Jesus noted that the use of many words does not enable the Father to hear more effectively. The point is that our Father already knows our needs before we present them. There is no need to give God a grocery list of concerns.

With this mini lesson on prayer, the disciples decided that they wanted to know how to pray. Jesus then proceeded to provide for the disciples a model prayer that begins with this sentence: "Our Father in heaven, hallowed be your name" (Matthew 6:9b). It is this sentence that is the focus of our further reflections.

Jesus cogently indicated that the disciples were to direct their prayers to God, who is our Father, the Creator of heaven and earth and all humankind. He told the disciples how to address God in prayer. The words of the prayer keep us focused on who we are and who God is. In doing this, Jesus illustrated and defined our relationship with God as well as our relationship with one another. This is a relationship of love. God loves each one of us and invites us to love our neighbors as we love ourselves.

It is not unusual for pilgrim disciples to wonder about the nature of prayer and the practice of prayer. In the Lord's Prayer, Jesus provides basic advice on how to pray. His words actually encourage us to engage in the art and practice of prayer.

Let us now consider the exact words of the text.

"Our"

Notice that the prayer begins with the word *our*, which is a corporate word, giving the prayer a sense of community. There is a sense of belonging and mutual sharing. Jesus did not say to pray, "*My* father." Community has to do with that which is mutual in nature and shared in responsibility.

There is no room for isolationism or playing the role of a loner. Jesus himself was never a loner, because he surrounded himself with twelve disciples whom he trained to do the work of ministry in partnership with him and the Holy Spirit.

God is not a possession belonging to any individual Christian. Quite to the contrary, Jesus presents God as our Father. On the one hand, God is my Father, but, on the other hand, God is our Father (yours and mine). Yes, I believe that God is my Father; however, God is not my Father alone. No one of us is an only child in relationship to God. God has many children, and all of us are God's children.

Consider a parent who has four children. This parent is father or mother to each one. The loving parent treats the children with equal love, with no distinction. There are four children in my primary family. Our parents loved each one of us with the same portion of love and acceptance. There was never any doubt in my mind about this abundant love.

It is refreshing and stimulating to know that the Lord's Prayer invites the one praying into a larger arena of living—the community of believers. The larger community is our family. It is our church family. It is the family of all God's children, which includes our brothers and sisters in the neighborhood and beyond to include the nations of the world.

As pilgrim disciples, we are members of the body of Christ. Following the Pauline imagery of the body of Christ, we are reminded that no one part of the body is any more important than another part. All members of the body have a purpose, function, and use. All the parts of the body are interrelated and they are dependent on one another. As members of the body of Christ, we pray with other pilgrim disciples in our public prayers and in our private prayers. We are the children of God. As the children of God, we have a Father.

"Our Father"

As human beings, we each have a biological father. This biological father may or may not be present in the life experiences of his children. It is problematic when a father is absent, especially in the case of boys. To be sure, both sons and daughters accrue great benefits from the parental presence of their fathers and the relationships that occur when a father is present in the home.

We know that some children do not know their fathers by name and experience because their fathers abandoned them in infancy. Some children lose their fathers to death. Some children do not know their natural fathers because they were adopted. These children experience a sense of loss in varying degrees.

We also know that some children do not have good feelings about their fathers because they were victims of abuse (sexual, physical, or psychological) at the hands of their fathers. Such experiences are carried in the psyche for a lifetime and can be coped with only through therapy and personal faith. Quite frankly, to address God as "Father" might be offensive to some people. Some scholars have suggested that the term *Father* meant "householder" during the time of Jesus. Yet, some of us have to overcome parental separation or other obstacles in order to claim God as Father.

How does one perceive God? How do you experience God? Perhaps one's attitude toward God and perception of God is skewed by one's experiences with one's own natural father.

Jesus invites us to go to God in prayer, to address God as Father, and to know God as Father. Jesus grants all of us permission to address God as Our Father. Such an intimate relationship with God is awesome, because it transcends all past experiences and provides a new orientation and foundation for facing the future. In such a prayerful relationship with God, we encounter God's intimate love for us.

God, according to John's Gospel, loved the world so much that God gave us God's Son. This was done so that believers in Jesus would not perish but would be able to have eternal life (see John 3:16). This is descriptive of God's unequivocal love and affection for humankind.

First John 4:14 says, "And we have seen and do testify that the Father has sent his Son as the Savior of the world." God sent Jesus because of God's love for us. Then we read in 1 John 4:16b, "God is love, and those who abide in love abide in God, and God abides in them." Our love is always deficient, but God expresses perfect love. God gives us the opportunity to claim this love.

The parable of the Prodigal and his Brother (Luke 15:11-32) helps us comprehend God's extravagant love in a practical situation of life. The story is about a father who had two sons. The younger son asked his father to advance to him his share of the anticipated inheritance. The father acquiesced, and the young man gathered his belongings and inheritance and traveled to a distant country. It was party time when he arrived at his destination. It was not long, however, before he lost all of his possessions. A famine hit the land, and the young man hired himself out to a local farmer who put him to work feeding the pigs. After becoming homeless, the young man decided to go home to his father. Now, it took a whole lot of courage, heaped up, to go home.

When he arrived at home, full of remorse and self-pity, the young man encountered a pleasant surprise. His father ran out to meet him and greeted him with a big hug and a father's kiss. His father had compassion for his son and showered him with joy and love. He even threw a party for his son. This story is about the love of a father, and that's the way it is with God's love.

The father loved his party-time son in the same way that he loved the elder stay-at-home son. Whether they stayed at home or left home, the father had an equal amount of love for each son.

God, the Father, is a forgiving Father. Jesus himself turned to his Father and asked God to forgive his accusers, mockers, captors, and executioners. Jesus offered forgiveness to one of the criminals who were sentenced to die beside him. We have a loving God who is a forgiving God. There is a place for all of God's children, and we address him as Father.

You may have certain issues with your earthly father. Such issues tend to create a deficit in terms of one's attitude toward our Heavenly Father. If there is a deficit, how do you fill it? Such a reality requires a faith response that begins and ends with "Our Father." Faith fills the deficit in response to God's love.

"Our Father in Heaven"

Our Father's home is in heaven. Jesus tells us this. On one occasion, Jesus tells his disciples that there are many mansions in his Father's house. Where is this house? How do we get there? How do we even know the way? Jesus said, "I am the way, and the truth, and the life" (John 14:6). Jesus is the way to his Father, who rules heaven and earth. God's house has space for all of God's children.

"Hallowed Be Your Name"

In everyday life, people refer to their fathers in a a variety of ways: Daddy, Pops, Papa, Pappy, Pa, and Old Man. In my family we called our father *Daddy*, then *Dad* when we became adults. People also describe fathers with such terms as "a good daddy," "a great pop," "a dear papa," "a wonderful pappy," "a loving pa," or "a gracious old man." We tend to describe our fathers in terms of our experience with them.

The reality is that we cannot perceive of God the Father except through the lens of our own eyes and the confines of our experiences. We see God, in part, as we see our own earthly fathers. This image may be positive or negative, or even neutral. Nevertheless, we are bound by the limitations of our experiences and culture.

The Lord's Prayer portrays the Father as "hallowed." To *hallow* God's name is to honor God: "hallowed be your name." The word *hallowed* means sacred, holy, sanctified, blessed consecrated, and deified. Only the name of God is treated with such honor. Jesus bids us to recognize the holiness of God's name.

Conclusion

We have a God who loves us more than we could ever imagine. As a matter of fact, God's love is nothing short of extravagant. "For God so loved the world that he gave his only Son, so that everyone who believes in him may not perish but may have eternal life" (John 3:16). God, out of abundant love, takes care of all God's children, in the good times and in the difficult times. We trust God because God is trustworthy. We honor God because God is worthy of our praise. This is why we address God as Our Father. I honor God because I have found our God to be a wonderful Father. Amen.

Note

1. Cleavant Derricks, "Just a Little Talk with Jesus" (1937).

CHAPTER SIX
"Our Father"

Jonathan D. Keaton

"Father, I stretch my hands to Thee."[1]
—Charles Wesley

Judaism, Islam, and Christianity have been called Abrahamic religions or faiths. Why? Because Abraham is claimed as the "spiritual ancestor, the founding father of their faith."[2] When our Lord taught the crowd to pray, he expressed God's parentage in much broader terms. Not circumscribed by the worldview of any religion or stifled by the unbelief of atheists or agnostics, Jesus declared that his father was "Our Father." That said, why would anyone hearing Jesus' admonition on prayer want to claim God as our Father?

It's What We've Been Taught

My mother and grandmother said when I was growing up that going to church, getting an education, being good, and especially believing in God were important. Believing in God meant accepting God as a Heavenly Father. If I had any doubt, words of Scripture were summoned as affirmation. Locked in my mind is a telling excerpt from Psalm

100:3 (KJV). "Know ye that the LORD he is God: it is he that hath made us, and not we ourselves; we are his people, and the sheep of his pasture."

In the fifties, my home church drove this traditional concept of God into our minds with an introit sung at the beginning of every worship service: "The Lord is in His Holy Temple: let all the earth keep silent before Him."[3] Therefore, we lived as children of God—subject to God's rules, beneficiaries of God's protection, exemplars of God's grace and mercy—bound in relationship with God forever. Truthfully, we came to belief based on what we were taught, not necessarily because we believed it ourselves. Our parents or some significant other said so; and that was that. Embracing God as "Our Father" came later.

Believing and accepting what people tell us is quite common. Their truth becomes our truth. For instance, Americans honor the contributions of the late Dr. Thomas A. Dorsey. From an outstanding music career singing, playing, composing blues and jazz, Dorsey turned to gospel music. The shift to gospel music was a direct result of the tragic death of his first wife and child. Dorsey is known as the "Father of Gospel Music."

In a similar vein, Dr. Carter G. Woodson is known as the "Father of Black History Month." Woodson dedicated his entire life to combating stereotypes, misinformation, and the notion that blacks have no history worth knowing. His lifelong efforts resulted in the creation of Black history and Black History Month. More important, his determination and research documented the countless ways Black Folk made the world a better place. To honor the historic nature of Woodson's contribution to American life, an ornament of Carter G. Woodson hangs on the White House Christmas Tree every year.[4]

Most Americans are familiar with the name of George Washington. He is known as the Father of America. Washington's achievements as a war hero, consummate politician, and public servant elected unanimously as the first President of the United States are reasons why George Washington has such an august title.

And yet, our acceptance of Dorsey, Woodson, and Washington as significant father figures comes by hearing, accepting, or reading the words of others who say "they are who they say they are." Thus, the crowd gathered for the Sermon on the Mount learns about God the way I did. When our Lord teaches them to pray, he asks his audience to accept what he teaches, namely that God is their Father.

It's Personal and Communal

In September of 2010, I led a cabinet retreat in the Grand Traverse District. A lay couple had invited the bishop and cabinet to utilize accommodations on their farm. How they served us gave full expression to a popular term in church growth literature called "radical hospitality." Where we stayed, what we ate, the meeting room, recreation possibilities, and every need was attended to by Joan and Jay Hook. Their serving was so complete and genuine, so joyful and fulfilling that one cabinet member named Robert Hundley quipped, "I feel like going from a Hundley to a Hook."[5] We laughed. But his quip was easily understood. The love and service extended to Bob felt like the treatment a son would receive. Every cabinet member including the bishop drew the same conclusion.

Herein lies a dual aspect of the claim that God is "Our Father." To believe in and pray to God whom we address as our Father means no religion, race, or nation has exclusive rights on God. God is to be shared as are God's blessings. Praying the Lord's Prayer, we ask God to provide food, avoidance of temptation, and deliverance from evil. More important, we place our need for forgiveness on a communal and conditional basis. Forgiveness or the lack thereof occurs only as we are willing to forgive others. What God does for one child of God, God willingly does for all.

When 700,000 tons of rock entombed thirty-three miners in Chile on August 5, 2010, prayers for their safe return were said worldwide. Petitions to God increased seventeen days later when it was discovered that all the miners had survived. And it took a new form. Rescuers from sixty-nine nations provided technical, scientific, medical, financial, political, manpower, and other assistance for the buried miners. When the thirty-three Chilean miners were raised from their rocky tomb one at a time over twelve hours the world watched and prayed for them, not just Chileans. We wanted God on their side. And God was.

At the same time, God operated at a personal level. Every rescued miner had a testimony about God saving them from a rocky tomb. Each miner wore a T-shirt over his uniform. On the front, it said, "Thanks Be to God." On the back of the shirt, an excerpt of Psalm 95:4 was emblazoned. "In his hand are the depths of the earth; the heights of the mountain are his also." A miner named Mario Sepulveda got a lot of attention from the worldwide audience as he neared the surface. People heard him shouting. Mario bounded out of the rescue capsule passing out souvenirs, as in rocks. The media ate that up. For a moment in time, Mario became the face of the rescued miners. However, what the media made secondary could not be quashed. Sepulveda declared that the mine explosion had produced a test of faith, that is, an immediate conversation and reaching out to God to be saved. Quite frankly, it had happened to every miner. That aside, Mario told the media about his personal encounter with God. "I was with God and the devil. They fought over me but God won. He took me by my best hand, the hand of God, and I held on to him."[6]

The testimonies of Robert Hundley and Mario Sepulveda show what God is like... "God knows what we need before we ask him" (see Matthew 6:8) and provides it. The Hooks prepared for our coming. They went the second and third mile to bless and care for us. They invited other persons from a friendship group to serve us a special meal. And they secured their son's house to use during our stay. They met and anticipated virtually every need we had and addressed it. In so doing, they evoked praise that we could not adequately put in words. Somewhat like Lazarus, Mario received a second chance. God's act of salvation enabled forty-year-old Mario to go home to his wife and two children with a renewed sense of the goodness of God. Plus, it provided an opportunity for Mario to testify about his present and future relationship with God.

In using the two stories, we have identified some of the ideas and human experiences Jesus' hearers might have imagined as they heard his sermon. Jesus offered advice for living summed up in the Golden Rule: love God and love neighbor. Those who chose to establish a relationship with Jesus found in him health, strength, and a friend for life. Joseph Scriven put it this way. We forfeit "peace" and "bear needless pain" in our lives because we're reluctant to "carry everything to God in prayer."[7]

It's About Jesus' Witness

Five times, before and after the Lord's Prayer and in the Sermon on the Mount (Matthew 5–7), our Lord paints a portrait of his Father. Plus, Jesus assumes that his Father is his listeners' Father.

Matthew 5:16: "Let your light shine before others, so that they may see your good works and give glory to your Father in heaven."

Matthew 5:48: "Be perfect, therefore, as your heavenly Father is perfect."

Matthew 6:1: "Beware of practicing your piety before others in order to be seen by them; for then you have no reward from your Father in heaven."

Matthew 6:14: "If you forgive others their trespasses, your heavenly Father will also forgive you."

Matthew 7:21: "Not everyone who says to me, 'Lord, Lord,' will enter the kingdom of heaven, but only the one who does the will of my Father in heaven."

Bottom line, Jesus suggests to the crowd that *God is the best model to live by*. The impact of this way of life is extant in some contemporary narratives.

1. A group of four- to eight-year-olds was asked, "What does love mean?" A four-year-old boy remembered a random act of kindness after his elderly neighbor lost his wife. "Upon seeing the man cry, he went next door, climbed up in the man's lap and sat there. When his mother asked him what he said to the old man, the little boy said, 'Nothing, I just helped him cry.' "[8] The boy let his light shine.
2. Most anyone would admit to the impossibility of being perfect or becoming perfect. Yet John Wesley's concept of perfection is alive and well in United Methodism's doctrine and polity. Every time this bishop conducts an annual conference service of ordination, I examine the candidates with a number of historic questions. One question reads thusly, "Are you going on to perfection?"[9]
3. When Joe Frazier died of liver cancer November 7, 2011, news media recalled the historic battles between him and Muhammed Ali in and outside the boxing ring. The historic taunts exchanged by Frazier and Ali over the years made forgiveness a remote possibility. Although both men offered apologies to each other, a cordial relationship never developed. Jesus shared a different approach to fixing fractured relationships. Instead of carrying a grudge or hating one's enemy, one ought to love them (Matthew 5:43-44). Christ modeled that behavior.

The night before his assassination, Martin Luther King preached his famous "I've Been to the Mountaintop" sermon at the Church of God in Christ headquarters in Memphis, Tennessee. The congregation heard about the history of past civilizations, the rise of mass movements for freedom around the world, the civil rights movement in America and Memphis, and how the Son of God called the people of God to a higher standard of behavior, individually and corporately. King shared his desire for long life, but emphasized that doing God's will was his major focus.[10] That is exactly what Jesus requested of those who dared to respond to the Lord's Prayer integrally. Do God's will!

A first-century narrative provided foundation for those above. When Jesus began his public ministry in Nazareth at his hometown synagogue, he embraced a mission that cared for everybody regardless of race, rank, or gender, child or adult, saint or sinner. The spirit of God, that is, of his Father, had sent him "to bring good news to the poor... to proclaim release to the captives and recovery of sight to the blind, to let the oppressed go free, to proclaim the year of the Lord's favor" (Luke 4:18-19). In essence, Jesus' behavior moved the crowd beyond a cognitive understanding of the Lord's Prayer. He was already doing what he asked of his hearers, word and deed.

Finally, our Lord did not ask the crowd if they would accept God as their heavenly Father. He declared that God was their Father and ours. And his hearers were free to accept or reject that reality. Yet, I believe most people accepted his message. God had the power to create the abundant life on earth for nations and for people. And God sent his Son to be the Messianic presence in the world—to save it by precept and example. Plus, God sent the power and inspiration of the Holy Spirit into the world so that every generation might sense the living presence of a God who is truly with us. That is the divine hope for all God's children.

Conclusion

When the sermon began, I asked the question "Why would anyone hearing Jesus' admonition on prayer want to claim God as our Father?" Yes, it's about what we have been taught; it's personal and communal; and it's about Jesus' witness. But most important, it's what we have learned about God through the corridors of time. Pure and simple, it pays to do what God asks. Is this not abundantly clear in the commandment (Exodus 20:12 KJV): "Honour thy father and thy mother: that thy days may be long upon the land which the LORD thy God giveth thee"?

The epigraph for this chapter reads, "Father, I stretch my hands to Thee." Although it is hardly sung in the Black Church now, the "old folks" used this Charles Wesley hymn to cry out to God in prayer. God was a Father who could always be called on in the time of trouble. He delivered. He answered prayer. Their heavenly Father had brought them from a mighty long way. Their heavenly Father had watched over them in sickness and in sorrow, through slavery, Jim Crow, and racism, through the freedom rides, boycotts, and marches on Washington, the births and deaths of children and loved ones, through unemployment and spates of prosperity. They honored a heavenly Father who heard petitions expressing the hopes, dreams, and longings of Black Folk—deferred far too often. Sung and prayed in the Black idiom—recalling to mind burdens lying on the souls of Black Folk—the words of the first verse routinely elicited outstretched hands, quiet moans, verbal shouts, noticeable rocking, weeping, powerful reflections, and spontaneous exclamations of "Lord, have mercy!" What was sung from the heart was being prayed from the heart for one and all. Memories of such pleadings—some of which I have done—flood my head, fill my heart, and flush my eyes. Right now, I can literally hear the church singing:

Father, I stretch my hands to Thee,
No other help I know;
If Thou withdraw Thyself from me,
Ah! whither shall I go?[11]

Amen.

Notes

1. Charles Wesley, "Father, I Stretch My Hands to Thee," *Songs of Zion* (Nashville: Abingdon Press, 1981), 11. See Matthew 6:7-9; Luke 11:2.
2. Allison Stokes, "Shalom, Salaam," Peace 2006 Women's Division, General Board of Global Ministries, 1.
3. The introit is based on Habakkuk 2:20.
4. http://www.nc.nrcs.usda.gov/about/blacksepm/index.html.
5. Many thanks to Robert Hundley and Jay Hook for permission to share this story.
6. http://content.usatoday.com/communities/Religion/post/2010/10/chile-mine-rescue-god-devil-sepulveda/1 (accessed November 2, 2011).
7. Joseph M. Scriven, "What a Friend We Have in Jesus," *The United Methodist Hymnal* (Nashville: The United Methodist Publishing House, 1989), 526. Used by permission.
8. http://www.articlescopy.com/quotWhat-Does-Love-Meanquot-See-How-4-8-Year-Old-Kids-Describe-Love/a7839_1.
9. *The Book of Discipline of the United Methodist Church, 2008* (Nashville: The United Methodist Church, 2009), ¶336.2.
10. See http://www.americanrhetoric.com/speeches/mlkivebeentothemountaintop.htm.
11. Wesley, "Father, I Stretch My Hands to Thee," verse 1.

CHAPTER SEVEN
Father at His Best

Ernest S. Lyght & Jonathan D. Keaton

When we look back at the preceding chapters, a dominant theme emerges. Most of what we write supports positive African American fathers, father figures at home and in church. Also, when we speak of *fatherhood*, we are not talking about the notion "father knows best," as depicted in the 1940s and 1950s radio and television comedy series. We are talking about "Father at his best." It is not a matter of a father knowing what is best. Rather, it is the case of African American fathers being their collaborative best in the practice of fatherhood. As it takes a village to raise a child, so it takes mother, extended family, the church, the community, and God to help Black fathers be the best they can be.

Whether a father is at home or a child is raised without a father, every child needs a father or father figure. Ideally, we would prefer that the father figure be the natural father. Divorce, untimely deaths due to car accidents, war, illnesses, abandonment, and incarceration deplete the ranks of fathers in the home. But in the resulting void, other men step forward to help—stepfathers, grandfathers, uncles, big brothers, neighbors, mentors, teachers, and preachers.

Even so, such practice occurs in an American milieu that rarely presents African American fatherhood as normative or health filled. The positive, the good, and the productive African American father is rarely seen nor heard. We beg to differ. When father is at his collaborative best, good things happen in the Black community.

In the Family

First, father at his best loves and supports his family.

Love and support are two of the most important gifts a father provides for his family. Refrains about love and support appear time and again in the witness and testimonies of families positively affected by Dad's love. Some speak of their father as loving and caring. Others cite a particular characteristic, such as "talkative" or "having a quiet strength." Some family members point to signal events or emotions as partial descriptors of the abiding relationship between father and child. For instance, the late Mrs. Dorothy Casey, a member of Bishop Keaton's church, told him that her father's love sustained her through many of life's difficulties. The late John H. Johnson bequeathed his publishing empire to adopted daughter Linda Johnson Rice. She learned to run the business working closely with her dad.[1] Linda Johnson Rice's father loved and trained his adopted daughter, like Christie Hefner, to be more than "Daddy's girl." And he succeeded. Bishop Lyght captured a son's love for his father using a few adjectives and ways of addressing his father in chapter 2, "I Remember": "I recall my dad with warm affection and fond memories" (page 19). "When we children got hurt, we always went to Dad for first-aid treatment" (page 20). "Dad was a mentor for me in ministry" (page 26).

As fathers, we know the importance and value of providing economic support for our families. Our children are grown. They have college degrees. Some of them are married with children. And the economic support continues via grandchildren and other financial concerns that may arise in the lives of our grown children. Economic support from father in no way suggests that families avoid want. Vast numbers of employed fathers constitute the "working poor." In essence, they do not make enough to care for the basic needs of the family much less pay for extras like proms, football games, music lessons, and, yes, college expenses. Nevertheless, the love and support necessary for stable family life exists for a lifetime.

Second, father at his best celebrates and affirms motherhood.

Dig through the historical notes and stories of numerous families, churches, and civil and human rights movements, and you will find mothers and mother figures playing major roles in every aspect of African American life. For that enduring contribution, they are cherished and loved. Within and outside the home, mothers can and do wield a great deal of influence: persons like Rosa Parks, Coretta Scott King, Bishop Leontine T. Kelly, First Lady Michelle Obama, Sojourner Truth, Harriet Tubman *aka* Black Moses, thousands of mothers who raise families, advocate for human rights, "woman" picket lines, teach, preach, and lead in every phase of life with the collaborative support of Black fathers. Often, due to the absence or dearth of men, mothers have been forced to lead by necessity. Because of her ministry to all God's children in the city of Fort Smith, Arkansas, in particular and the state of Arkansas in general, Euba Mae Harris-Winton, a Black Community Developer with the General Board of Global Ministries of The United Methodist Church, was named one of the ten matriarchs of Arkansas in 1989.[2] Her commendation of service was widely acclaimed by men and women across the state.

Third, father at his best functions as a father figure for others.

Because matriarchal families are a major aspect of African American life, men in every type of family function as fathers. Depending on the circumstances, grandfathers, uncles, nephews, cousins, stepfathers, or persons successful in making a living will be called on to be present, to be a role model, to provide an example, to adopt a child, to offer financial support on a one-time or daily basis. In order to continue the African American family from generation to generation, these steps have been necessary. And we note that the Black Church and the Black preachers have been both father and mother to the African American family.

Fourth, father at his best values African American heritage.

Most African Americans understand when written or spoken language includes code words. It is as natural as breathing. Writing about the early years, in chapter 2, Bishop Lyght reflects:

> Every now and then when I was growing up, Dad would tell me that he did not want me to have to go through what he went through when he was growing up and working to become a responsible adult. Life for him was difficult by every standard. He shouldered certain family burdens while striving to reach his goals in life. (page 21)

Clearly, being a responsible adult and a good father, husband, and pastor were wonderful goals that the Rev. William Lemuel Dewey Lyght pursued.

Yet, this quotation calls to mind what every person in America knows. Though our parents wish their children did not have to go through certain things, generation after generation knows that will not be the case. Dr. King expressed the sentiment in his "I Have a Dream" speech. King hoped that all children would one day live in a land where their character would be more important than their skin color.

That day has not arrived. DuBois offered the same truth noting "the problem of the twentieth century is the problem of the color line."[3] Because of this second-class sentiment embedded in American culture, African American fathers and mothers work overtime instilling positive images in their children. Here are a few examples: "You are not less than; you are as good as"; "God didn't make 'no junk'"; "As a man thinketh so is he"; "Accept your African

American heritage as a gift from God"; "Don't let other folk define you." We said as much to our children and equipped them accordingly. Father at his best is in constant dialogue and relationship with his sons, daughters, and extended family correcting negative images, offering positive feedback, and functioning as a positive role model so that his children see that his walk and talk are consistent.

In the Church

First, father at his best is a person of religious faith.[4]

Many women seeking marriage partners look for a man who loves them, has a job, would be a good father, and is a responsible citizen. Another very important essential may be religious compatibility or that her husband to be is a man of religious faith. Marriage, child rearing, supporting the family, and developing a healthy family life are enhanced if Dad turns to God, wife, and significant others for help. An old saying with staying power lives among us. "A family that prays together stays together." Given the challenge of making a living, finding a job, and addressing the challenges that impinge on the lives of African Americans, fatherhood requires a "faith that will not shrink, though pressed by every foe."[5]

Second, father at his best utilizes the church as a supportive community for his parenting role.

When we compared notes concerning our upbringing in the Black Church, a number of parallels surfaced. The Black Church shaped our faith and inspired us to value our community, education, and self. Both of us learned about faith in God and the value of community and education. Last but certainly not least, the Black Church taught us to be leaders. Hardly an Easter program was held that we did not have a part to memorize and perform. Reports were given at Sunday school and engagement in dialogue was expected.

Not only did we participate in Methodist Youth Fellowship, we served as officers. Participation in district and conference meetings was expected as well. As more and more church members identified us as persons who ought to think about a career in ministry, all that we did and said inside and outside the church had to demonstrate that we were the kind of persons who had the family background, the temperament, and the leadership aptitude to be ministers of the gospel, should we be called. Both of us were called. And we accepted. Yet without the clear expectation from home that participation in church was non-negotiable, our deep involvement in the church from the day of our birth till now most likely would not have happened.

Third, father at his best is a father figure in the body of Christ.

Though we grew up in homes where one father was present (Bishop Lyght's father) and the other absent (Bishop Keaton's dad), both of us benefitted from father figures in the church. Because of their Christian stature, male presence, and mentoring relationship, these men helped to shape our maturation as young men, children of God, and participants in the ministry of all Christians. One example of such empowerment can be gleaned from some of the father figures in Bishop Keaton's home church in Ft. Smith, Arkansas. His experiences are paradigmatic of what happens in the Black Church.

Pastors of Mallalieu. Every pastor that served Mallalieu, I knew personally. Mama (my grandmother) had them out to the house for dinner regularly. Both Mother and Mama expected the pastors to get their children involved and keep us involved in the ministry of the church. Every time the doors of the Church opened, my siblings and I were there. Every pastor asked me if God was calling me into ministry.

Laymen of Mallalieu. Sergeant Washington was a retired soldier. The grownups called him Unc—we never did. We addressed him by his retired title. His wife ran the

Father at His Best

Methodist Youth Fellowship. Sergeant Washington got involved with the youth in the summer. He drove us to Camp Aldersgate in Little Rock, Arkansas. Besides being an affirming male presence, Sergeant Washington taught me the value of persistence and being constant in season and out. On our drives to Little Rock, he often commented on cars that passed us in a hurry. "If we keep a steady beat," he said, "we'll see some of them again." Sure enough, we did. When he died years later, his wife flew me to South Carolina to preach his funeral. At the funeral, I told the audience how that lesson impacted other parts of my life.

Cleo Wesson ran a barber shop in downtown Ft. Smith, Arkansas. He gave me a job as a shoeshine boy and janitor in his shop.

Mr. Cox, a retired principal, showed me how he and his wife got along in their marriage of more than sixty years. I witnessed firsthand how he loved his wife and cared for others. Mrs. Cox hired me to perform chores like cleaning the house, doing yard work, baking cakes, and so on.

When I desperately needed $75 dollars to stay in college, Dr. McDonald let me have it on a promise of repayment. When I tried to pay him back, Dr. McDonald refused to take the money, saying, "Do it for somebody else." I remember to this day that timely loan by the doctor in my home church.

Chaplain Easley, an Army chaplain who joined Mallalieu Methodist Episcopal Church, had me involved in prison ministry as a young boy. On assignment at the army stockade, Chaplain Easley conducted services for prisoners every Sunday. For a year, I played the piano in the service of worship led by Chaplain Easley. For playing, I earned about $7.00 a Sunday.

These and countless other stories dramatize the value, place, and role father figures played in Bishop Lyght's and Bishop Keaton's growth and development in the faith of Jesus Christ and his church.

Fourth, father at his best addresses the plight of absent fathers in the home.

First, as bishops of The United Methodist Church, we've been asked to write letters of commendation for young men in our area who have become Eagle Scouts. No higher rank than Eagle Scout can be attained in the Boy Scouts of America. Usually, recipients have earned many merit badges, performed with distinction acts of kindness that are in harmony with the Scout motto, law, and ethos. They have demonstrated leadership, vision, planning, and involvement to complete a major service project designed to serve others. Men who get involved in scouting ministries extend themselves beyond their own families to train young men as responsible men, citizens, and future fathers. Other ministries supported by the local church such as United Methodist Men, Big Brothers programs, camping, golf outings, or fishing trips have given fathers of families opportunities to be present for other men's children whose fathers are absent. They provide resources for children to go to camp, or they are present for children who desire a simple heart-to-heart conversation with a father figure.

Second, some churches have held conferences on the plight of the Black male or the Black family. Attending and leading workshops on keeping young men in school, decreasing the rate of unwed pregnancies, training young fathers to accept responsibility for their children, encouraging them to use the resources of the church, or strengthening their faith provide additional opportunities for fathers to positively affect the lives of children beyond their families.

Third, before and after he retired, Dr. Zan Holmes made a practice of visiting a local church and a correctional center in the East Ohio Annual Conference. That church took the *Disciple* Bible study into prisons. Most of the African American inmates who took the study were doubly inspired: they met one of the presenters of the study who looked like them, and they changed their lives for the better inside and beyond the prison walls.

Fourth, as bishops and fathers, we have been led to address numerous concerns and issues facing the whole church and the Black Church in particular. In addition to being family role models, we have accepted the challenge of putting some of our thoughts on paper with the idea that we might make some positive contribution to the notion of father at his best.

Conclusion

Some of our readers may wonder why this book focuses on father at his best. There are many reasons, but one stands above all. In word and deed, television, radio, Internet, and common discourse, we hear *ad nauseum* about the Black father at his worst. Both kinds of fathers have always existed, but good, responsible African American fathers rarely make the news. So we are adding to the scarce pile of literature that dares to focus, praise, and affirm the Black father at his best. Linda Johnson Rice, CEO of Johnson Publishing Company, strikes this note talking about the focus of *Ebony* and *Jet* magazines: "We are not here to pick apart African Americans. We are here to celebrate and uplift and inspire."[6]

To be sure, "Father at his best" is a relative term. Depending on one's point of view, one child's best parent is another's good, average, or great parent. We are aware that a variety of father figures are constantly making positive contributions to the lives of Black families. The cumulative effect of these interventions enables children without fathers in the home to reap some positive benefit from a caring relationship with that father figure. At the same time, we are aware that presence alone at home does not automatically translate into healthy ways of caring and loving children or tending to their needs. Nevertheless, we do know by experience that fathers and father figures are beneficial to children.

Finally, we honor the contributions of Black fathers because we believe the biblical injunction is right. "Honor your father and your mother, so that your days may be long in the land that the LORD your God is giving you" (Exodus 20:12). Are we not under obligation from God to honor both parents? Why God embraces honoring parents when "all have sinned and fall short of the glory of God" (Romans 3:23) is a paradox. Given this divine paradox, we have chosen to honor Black fathers in this work. We believe it is the right thing to do. Having been blessed to live three score years plus more as fathers ourselves, we have concluded that our witness can and will strengthen, help, and encourage Black fathers in their current practice of fatherhood. If that be the case, we will not have written in vain!

Notes

1. Shashank Bengali, "Jetsetter," *USC Trojan Family Magazine* (Winter 2002). http://uprserver4.usc.edu/trojan_family/winter02/jetsetter.html (accessed November 2, 2011).

2. "Matriarchs Make Their Mark," *Arkansas Gazette* (September 24, 1989, Section E). Mrs. Winton was among ten honorees commended "for making Arkansas a better place to live." Some of her involvements included second vice president of the NAACP, vice president of the Fort Smith League of Women voters, treasurer of Arkansas Family Planning Council, member of Black Methodists for Church Renewal, Justice of the Peace, and more. Mrs. Winton is Bishop Keaton's mother.

3. William E. B. DuBois, *The Souls of Black Folk* (New York: Avon Books, 1965), 209.

4. See Edsel A. Ammons, Ernest S. Lyght, and Jonathan D. Keaton, *The Confessions of Three Ebony Bishops* (Nashville: Abingdon Press, 2008). Sketches of Bishop Lyght and Bishop Keaton's spiritual journeys are found on pages 11 and 23 respectively. In these word portraits, one can see the spiritual formation of each bishop occurring at home and in church.

5. William Hiley Bathurst, "O, for a Faith That Will Not Shrink" (1831).

6. Bengali, "Jetsetter."

Appendix A

Bishop Keaton's School Paper

Our Father, Where Are the Fathers?

Table of Contents
My parents ---- Page 1
My ancestors ---- Page 1
My sisters & brothers --- Page 1
Early school days --- Page 2
My first trip ---- Page 2
My first party ---- Page 2
My Best Friend ---- Page 3
The Most wonderful day --- Page 3
Christmas at our House --- Page 4
My likes and dislikes --- Page 4
Plans for the future --- Page 5

Appendix A

I, Jonathan Dayle Keaton, was born March 30, 1946, in Fort Smith, Arkansas.

My parents are Mr. and Mrs. John Keaton. My father only finished high school, but my mother did and went on to college. The college she attended was Philander Smith in Little Rock.

Rev. and Mrs. D. H. C. Harris are my grandparents. My grandfather once pastored the church I now go to. Now my grandfather is dead but my grandmother is still living. My maternal great, great, grandfather fought in the Civil War. There are others I cannot name so I will go on to tell you about some of my brothers and my sisters.

I have four sisters and three brothers. I am the third from being the eldest child. The others are either younger or older than I. A few of their names are Reginald, whose nickname is Reggie. Renella, her name is Toni. Most of the time we are on good terms with each other and at other times this is not so. Reggie is the youngest of all. He is always into something.

Toni is quiet and likes to stay at home and around most of the time.

Gwenetta and Vera are talkative and easy mostly to get along with. They also have good singing voices which is put to a lot of use at school and church.

(1.)

The first days of school found a new world for me. I learned the names of different boys and girls and also I got me a friend. My best friend was Jerry Johnson and I believe now that we are still best friends.

Our teachers we had at Catholic were called by a name such as sister so and so. They taught us what we were supposed to know etc. I'm sure they did their best and so will teachers to come. My present English teacher name is Mrs. Bullack.

My first trip was to Spiro, Oklahoma. There I went to visit someone along with my brothers and sisters. We stayed only about half a day. When we got there it was dusk and my sister had gone to sleep before we arrived there. She slept almost till we were ready to go back home. On the way back it rained. Fortunately we didn't have any accident or mishap to come our way.

The one party I have had was when I was about six or seven years old. I invited children in the neighborhood and I invited Jerry. My birthday cake was pink with all of that good icing on it. My name was written across the cake in icing. We did things people usually do at birthday parties such as played games, had refreshments, cake and other things. I got a few presents and money and things. We had a lot of fun at the party and I think everyone else enjoyed themselves. One party is all I've had chance to have but I know it is quite an experience to be able to have a party in one's lifetime. Because it certainly feels good to be on the receiving side once in awhile.

(2)

Appendix A

My best friend is Jerry Johnson. We have been friends since he and I have known each other, since we have have been in the kindergarten til now. I don't know what caused us to be so close and dear to each other. We would always share things together if we had anything the other one could have. We would always visit each other and each one's house. We have always mostly gotten along nicely, and we have never had anything such as arguments, misunderstandings to cause hard feelings among each other. I hope we will continue to be the way we have always been if not I don't know what will happen. That is the advantage of having a best friend. So you can share secrets, thoughts, and other things.

The most wonderful day that I have experienced is the day of a certain picnic. This picnic was joined together with others. There were different kinds of rides. We all played along together. They served refreshments free, also they served til they ran out. They had hot dogs, chocolate milk and drink, soda pop, ice cream, fudgesickles. They also gave away prizes of which I received none. This happened because I didn't have the right ticket. But I think this was one of the most enjoyable of days that I have experienced and know.

(3)

Our Father, Where Are the Fathers?

Christmas at our house is a joyous occasion. We wake up in the morning expecting to find gifts and things we have given each other. My sisters and brothers discover their toys and shout with the loudest glee. Christmas is the time of rejoicing because Jesus Christ is born. We have pecans, nuts, apples, oranges and different things. We eat breakfast and if they have church service we go to church. After that we might have dinner and they, the grownups, might go off and we could go, possibly. This is the way in which we spend our Christmas at home.

My likes and dislikes are great in number. I will first start with my dislikes for food. Cauliflower is one of my major dislikes so are cucumbers. I also dislike beets, hominy, and okra. Some of the foods I like are, lemon pie, cherry pie, apple pie, chocolate cake, strawberry shortcake, Devil's food and many others.

Some of the meats I like are, chicken, roast beef, turkey, hamburger meat, and also ham.

Chores I do around the house are cutting the yard, clean up my room, rake the yard

(4)

Appendix A

"My plans for the future are learning to become a doctor I think. If this does not satisfy me I will change to something else"

(5)

Appendix B

Bishop Keaton's Funeral Memoir

Appendix B

LAMENTING THE DEATH OF MY FATHER
Clinton "P. T." Keaton, Sr.

Born: July 15, 1927   Died: June 24, 1989

June 30, 1989

When I entered the church, no one was there in the sanctuary except me, my father, and God. The ushers and the undertakers were outside. The casket was open; so, I walked down the aisle to see him.

His presence startled and shocked me! I expected to see some resemblance between he and I. None seemed apparent. His skin was brown and mine light brown. His features seemed to be those of a distinguished gentleman, broadshouldered, well-dressed, gray mustache and hair of the same color, closely cut. When I looked at him, I felt strange. Here lay my father, but the relational and connectional ties were missing. So, I reached down and touched him. His body gave a little. Finished, I walked to the back of Ninth Street Baptist Church--to a section three or four rows from the back and sat down, looking forward at my father lying in state. Before I reached my father's casket initially, I saw a flag. He was a veteran of the U.S. Army. "What else was he?", I kept asking myself.

July 1, 1989

My thoughts were interrupted by Mr. Curtis Gilyard, over 70, one of the funeral home staff. He wanted to talk. And I talked with him, although I was irritated. I asked him what he

1

LAMENTING THE DEATH OF MY FATHER
Clinton "P. T." Keaton, Sr.

knew about my dad. I assumed he would tell me a lot, since they had been good friends for a long time. (Gilyard's opinion.) the most I got was they had worked together at the Goldman Hotel (it exists no longer). My dad left Ft. Smith years ago. Gilyard worried about the condition of his soul since, according to Gilyard, my father wasn't a churchgoer. Finally, I got away from him. Soon after, the family entered the church. (By then, I had taken a seat beside my mother.) As they filed in, I strained to see my brothers. They were stairsteps in height. Again, none resembled me. I did feel strange not being in the procession, and being ommitted from the program. The bulletin listed 5 sons; I was not mentioned. Being left out, however, did not make me angry. However, it was disappointing. As the family continued to file in, Leola and her children headed straight for me and sat down. Leola was the woman, years and years ago, who came to the house, put me on her bike, and took me to my grandparents' house. She also gave me a picture of my father some years ago. I hugged Leola as she sat down. Immediately, Leola asked me if I would sit with the family and her. I hesitated. "I'm not here to cause trouble, make a scene or anything", I explained. "I just wanted to be here--to witness my father's funeral. "Will you sit with me?", she asked. I said, "Yes." As I got up and walked with Leola and her family

2

Appendix B

LAMENTING THE DEATH OF MY FATHER
Clinton "P. T." Keaton, Sr.

to join the rest of the Keaton family, a surge of mixed emotion, as powerful as any I have felt before hit me. It took <u>all</u> the personal control within me not to burst into uncontrollable weeping. The weeping was due more to being <u>included</u>, recognized publicly after 43 years, than it was tears for my father. Years before, Leola had included me. Even now, she aggressively sought my inclusion. Leola sat beside me, held my hand when she thought it necessary, walked with me, linked arms with me, ever watching. I fought off tears during the reading of Psalm 90, the prayer by the pastor, and the singing of the song, "When I've Gone the Last Mile of The Way." During the meditation and for the rest of the service, I regained my inner composure. Nothing showed on the outside anytime. They rolled the casket to the back of the church. Leola took me by the arm and escorted me to the casket for the final reviewal. (Thirty to 40 minutes after I had just had my <u>first</u> look). I reached out and touched him again. I looked in his face for some sign, some message, some word. None came. So, I turned away and waited for Leola to pay her last respects. I linked arms with her; and we went down the steps together. Mother did not view the body, or go to the cemetery. She was working through and ending her own chapter with Clinton.

Outside, I met my brothers: Troy, Clinton, Jr., and David. David and I connected the most. He was sitting in a

LAMENTING THE DEATH OF MY FATHER
Clinton "P. T." Keaton, Sr.

stationwagon across the street. Unknowingly, he had parked right behind the car I had rented to drive into Ft. Smith from the Tulsa airport. Leola introduced me to him. Tall, dark and articulate <u>David</u>. When he learned that we were brothers--although it was a startling revelation--reached out and embraced me. That embrace tore down the divide of years for me--embrace from a stranger--embrace from my brother. Oh God, how could it be? It did not occur to me until this writing that there may have been something pre-ordained about our linkage since the Biblical David and Jonathan were soul mates. Leola, <u>my first cousin</u>, wanted to know if I was going to the cemetery. I said, "Yes". As I pulled out to join the funeral procession, David motioned for me to go in front of him. My car was third in the procession. En route to the cemetery, I cried again. Mother had chosen not to go, so I was alone. When we arrived, Leola rushed to my side again. We heard the brief graveside service. I wished that I were conducting it instead of Reverend Parrish. An American flag was presented to the family with thankfulness for Clinton "P. T.", Sr's service to the government and country. Shortly thereafter, I greeted my brother again, secured phone numbers and learned that David joined a fraternity I had joined in college, Alpha Phi Alpha. Clinton, Jr., briefly reviewed the last days of his father's life. He had been sick, had laid around the house until forced to go to the hospital

4

Appendix B

LAMENTING THE DEATH OF MY FATHER
Clinton "P. T." Keaton, Sr.

by Clinton, Jr. He experienced intense pain--so much so that painkillers were ineffective. After kidney failure, Dad went on dialysis. Nothing worked. The rest of his systems broke down and so did his life June 24, 1989. It was rumored that he died of cirrhosis of the liver.

David Keaton, my uncle, talked to me at the gravesite. He expressed sadness of our having to come together in these circumstances. I agreed. At the same time, I told him that my father's death provided an opportunity for me to see my father, though deceased, and meet my brothers.

Thanks be to God for the wonderful gift handed me. Thanks be to God that all my rancor and bitterness over my father had long since been resolved, as I struggled to understand what my circumstance in life had and has been. Truly, I can resonate with the psalmist in Lamentation which stated:

> Remember my affliction and my bitterness
> the wormwood and the gall
> My soul continually thinks of it
> and is bowed down within me.
> But this I call to mind and
> therefore I have hope.
> The steadfast love of the Lord never ceases
> his mercies never come to an end
> they are new every morning,
> great is Thy faithfulness.

JDK/ld

Appendix C

Bishop Keaton's "Man in the Mirror" Article

Appendix C

MAN IN THE MIRROR
Michigan Christian Advocate Article
Bishop Jonathan D. Keaton

I was in Powell, Wyoming on June 25, 2009. I was one of the Study Leaders for the Spiritual Growth Study Food & Faith sponsored by the United Methodist Women at the Pacific Regional School of Christian Mission. And the word came like a thief in the night with no preamble "He's dead! Michael Jackson is dead!" CPR, skilled paramedics, UCLA's ER brass and prayer failed to resuscitate him. Globally, his fans wept. For Michael Jackson had connected with them. This bond went far beyond the adage "Gone too soon."

The next day, I announced Michael's death to the class. Some of them had not yet heard. Gasps turned to amazement as we read the first two sentences of the worship service printed in the textbook. It said, "Talking to the one in the mirror: Michael Jackson recorded a song called "Man in the Mirror" saying that he was talking to that man and telling him he had to change his ways." How ironic. A study guide written two years ago used a Jackson song to help us understand the Image of God.

And the song helped us discuss Michael's ups and downs. I shared a historical parallel citing John Newton, the author of Amazing Grace. Then, we viewed Man in the Mirror on the Internet. Tears flowed. Because of Michael's untimely death, we were challenged to hold up a mirror to our own lives and change. Near the end of class, the spirit moved. The youngest student interrupted our discussion and sang a few bars of Jackson's "I'll Be There" spontaneously. "You and I must make a pact; we must bring salvation back, where there is love, I'll be there." Those words and her gifted voice sounded like the plaintive cry of John the Baptist in the wilderness. "It cut me to the quick." Jackson's music and lyrics insisted on self-assessment, change and doing something positive for all God's people.

Michael Jackson touched the world because he dared to look in the mirror at his flaws. What he saw threatened to destroy him. A childhood lost, abject loneliness, the breakup of the Jackson Five, two failed marriages, lawsuits, trials and tabloid stories shaped his image and reputation. So did vitiligo, a skin disease. It turned his black skin, white. 2nd and 3rd degree burns sustained during a 1994 Pepsi commercial left him with charred skin and bald spots on his scalp. Skin grafts helped. However, nothing solved the physical and emotional pain in its wake. Yet every time Michael Jackson climbed on the stage to sing and dance for his global audience, his stumbling blocks became stepping stones. He was transformed. He "beat it." Nay, he "beat them," i.e., his troubles.

Singing and dancing weren't his only gifts. Michael became a consummate humanitarian. In essence, Michael Jackson sang and danced with such passion because it allowed him to serve and love the world. Reportedly, three to five hundred million dollars of his earnings were donated to heal the world. Jackson used his earnings to fight leukemia, child abuse, diabetes, burns, AIDS, poverty, and illiteracy. He provided funds for children's vaccines, cancer research, endowed entertainment scholarships, black colleges and the NAACP. Jackson made similar decisions in his will. 20% of his estate was set aside for worthy causes.

The last twelve years of Michael Jackson's life was most productive. He spent it parenting. As the sole parent, Michael Jackson raised and nurtured with love Prince Michael age 12, Paris Katherine, age 11 and Prince Michael II, age 7. Rev. Al Sharpton's powerful eulogy re-iterated that message. Sharpton told Michael Jackson's children that their daddy taught the world to love, to dream, to care for one another, to never give up and value family. Paris Katherine confirmed Sharpton's witness about her Dad with an unscripted testimony of her own. "Ever since I was born, daddy has been the best father you could ever imagine...I just wanted to say I love him so much." So said the tape I watched of the Jackson Memorial Service. It was wonderful. At times, it left me in tears.

Nevertheless, the stirring accounts of Jackson's life on stage brought back memories of the Spiritual Growth Study in Powell, Wyoming. Both the Study and Man in the Mirror had something in common: 1. the need to change things; 2. and the desire to make the word a better place. Furthermore, they stressed the following: needed change in our world must begin with you and me. That's the purpose of looking at the "Man/Woman in the Mirror."

Finally, I must confess the Jackson Memorial Service left me with a telling observation. For all his shortcomings, Michael Jackson made a lot of disciples in the last 40 years. They just kept growing in number all over the world. Why? Michael Jackson truly loved and served all God's children. Second, Michael Jackson reached out and made the world a better place. That said, even Michael Joseph Jackson did not fully understand how or why folk around the world loved him back.

CPSIA information can be obtained at www.ICGtesting.com
Printed in the USA
LVOW120733090212

267792LV00003B/3/P